SPIRITED

A FABRIC ARTIST'S PASSION FOR LIFE

THREADS

THE ART & WRITINGS OF
PATRICIA ROBERTS CLINE

Cynthia Grant Tucker

12/97

Patricia Roberts Cline with her Sampler Quilt, *December 1981*

SPIRITED

A FABRIC ARTIST'S PASSION FOR LIFE

THREADS

THE ART & WRITINGS OF
PATRICIA ROBERTS CLINE

CYNTHIA GRANT TUCKER

SIBYL
PUBLICATIONS
Portland, Oregon

Published by SIBYL Publications, Inc. • 1007 S.W. Westwood Drive • Portland, Oregon 97201 • (503) 293-8391 • (800) 240-8566

ISBN 0-9638327-8-6

Editor: *Marge Columbus*

Graphic Design: *Design Studio Selby*

6 5 4 3 2

Photo credits listed on page 256

Cataloging in Publication Data

Cline, Patricia Roberts.
     Spirited threads : a fabric artist's passion for life : the art & writings of Patricia Roberts Cline / [edited by] Cynthia Grant Tucker. -- 1st ed.
     p. cm.
     ISBN: 0-9638327-8-6

    1. Cline, Patricia Roberts--Diaries. 2. Quiltmakers--United States--Diaries. 3. Cystic fibrosis--Patients--United States--Diaries. I. Tucker, Cynthia Grant. II. Title.

TT140.C55A3 1997   746.46'092
                   QBI97-40570

Printed in Canada

CONTENTS

This book is for all the generations

of stitching and scribbling women whose

knowing hands are guiding ours,

and for Eddie Cline.

PREFACE

A boundless adventure was in the offing the afternoon in the early spring of 1995 when Patricia Cline, a talented textile artist and friend, consented to lend me her journals to turn into "some sort of book." It was just a few weeks before her fifty-second birthday, an amazing milestone for someone born with cystic fibrosis, a brutal disease that kills nearly all who are caught in its grip before their teens. For four or five years, as her illness had finally forced her onto oxygen and at last confined her to her bed, Pat had been keeping a private record of her life. I knew from the parts she had shared with me that her words carried all the veracity of those who have no time or breath to waste, and that they opened a window onto a realm where talent and wisdom and love were being refined in the fires of disability.

Intended for nobody's eyes but her own, Pat's journals were far less tidy than functional. They furnished safekeeping for all sorts of clippings and correspondence and a mixture of personal confidences and the artist's technical notes, which she generated while choosing her fabrics and working out complex quilting strategies. Her prose, rich and fluid, had also been licensed to do as it liked, particularly with punctuation and syntax. This is not uncommon for private writing, and yet the last thing we wanted was a book that might be regarded as a curiosity. Because our aim was to offer an engaging and readable work, I decided to edit firmly, yet preserve Pat's voice and intentions.

To this end, I freed her prose of distracting quirks and pared the content to roughly a third, in part by sifting the technical notes from the personal comments and using them for a studio talk at the end. In addition, I took out the tangents, as well as personal information that would have infringed on others' privacy. Sometimes, when such material's significance argued for keeping it, I gave it more general contours by leaving out names.

Out of respect for the readers' need for some distance, as much as for Pat's desire to keep some things closed off from public gaze, I also left parts of Pat's story vague by removing the particulars. Yet where her unspeakable secrets are told—along with her public triumphs—the writer fleshed out the terror and pain and excruciating indignities of the chronic disease that was slowly destroying her body. We believed that our telling her story would open the way for others to speak of their burdens, name their pain, and embrace their own imperfections.

This is not to minimize Pat's discomfort with having her private life put on display. Even after she learned that most of her secrets were not really secrets at all, but the whispered history that family members had long shared discreetly among themselves, she preferred not to see the painful details dredged up by her own hand and thereby accorded not only longevity, but a kind of distinction she felt they did not deserve. What fed a greater anxiety, though, was a fear of appearing always at her best, not her worst—or as something better. While protective of others' good names, she was haunted by the idea that she herself would be trotted out as a saint. Pat's worries about being stripped of her humanity and kinship with readers guided my hand and firmed my resolve to produce an honest book.

Affecting not only the text, but every aspect of our production, Pat's refusal to have her story romanticized also released us from other conventions that keep books from bringing their writers and readers together. When I first started planning this book, I imagined that as I slipped into the role of Pat's editor or biographer, I would also slip into the customary fiction of anonymity. It would appear that I was not present in either the journals or her life. My illusion that I would be able to pull this off easily was short-lived, however. Not a month after I had taken Pat's journals home and read them through, I sensed that something was bothering her and went over to learn what it was. Fighting off tears, she said that she had been leading me on by letting me think that she had actually led the exemplary life she supposed made me take such an interest. Hating to lose my respect and our friendship, she had not found the courage to tell me the truth before, but now her masquerade had become too unbearable and she was determined to tell me about her story's darker side. I was hardly prepared for such a confession after reading what she had recorded. But like most people who keep private notebooks over long stretches of time, she had rarely gone back to see what she had written before, and so when I stepped in and told her what she was about to tell me, she was shocked, and then hugely relieved. Relieved not only to learn that she had not hidden a thing from herself or from me, but that there had never been any need to do so. At that moment, when we felt the hand of grace stitching away, reinforcing the seams of our friendship, I realized how hard it was going to be to pretend that our roles had been separate.

Some months later Pat asked to read my diaries to see what sort of record I had been keeping. From that point on, our journal entries captured us not only visiting each other's lives in the present, but trekking through each other's recollections and reveling in our unorthodox meetings. It still took me a while to catch on, and until I did, in editing what Pat had written, I crossed out my name whenever I saw it until it came my turn for making confessions. When I told her what I had been doing—and tried to justify the tampering as a fear of inflating my role—she refused to buy it. I was part of her life, she insisted, and therefore obliged to appear or I would not only be falsifying her story but also abandoning her. And so I have written an opening essay and the closing words, and in Part II, I step in with transitional comments and clarification.

The dream of producing this book has become a reality in part through the generosity of the H.W. Durham Foundation, the Memphis Arts Council, and Target Stores' Innervision initiative to make the arts available to underserved members of the community, as well as through significant matching support from the University of Memphis. Our heartfelt thanks go to these organizations, as well as to Sibyl Publications and to all of the people whom we name at the end of this book for their roles in shaping its story. These friends have made it possible for me to learn this about quilting and books: Their truest measure is not to be found in the distance between their beginnings and endings, but in the strength of the seams that bind and sustain their relationships.

Cynthia Grant Tucker
Memphis, Tennessee

PART I: SISTER'S CHOICE

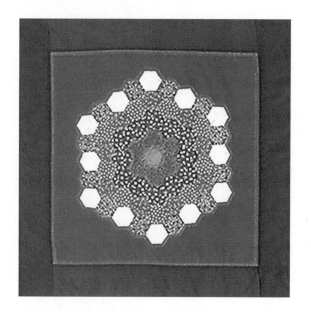

Motheroot

Creation often
needs two hearts
one to root
and one to flower
One to sustain
in time of drouth
and hold fast
against winds of pain
the fragile bloom
that in the glory
of its hour
affirms a heart
unsung, unseen.

—MARILOU AWIAKTA from
Selu: Seeking the Corn-Mother's Wisdom

Pat and Cynthia, March 1991

PART I:
SISTER'S
CHOICE

We are reading the novel *The Color Purple* and in it we notice Sofia and Celie outside on the porch. They have set up a quilting frame there and are piecing a top from scraps, some cut from an old yellow dress contributed to the venture by Shug, Celie's mentor. "It a nice pattern call Sister's Choice," Celie brags of the quilt in a letter to God. And aptly named, too, it turns out, as the characters' lives, once isolated and ragged, are slowly restored and enlarged through sisterly love. This picture of women and well-worn fabric transforming each other and being transformed has special significance for the intricate piecework of writings presented here. For Alice Walker's tableau was the germ of the conversations and friendship from which this volume has come to exist. And now that its threads of shared history have been worked into one mosaic, the image of Walker's women returns to us as an emblem of this book's witness. Like Celie's quilting, ours testifies to the redemptive power of women's words and their faithful collaboration.

In *Spirited Threads,* a cross between edited journals and memoir, the reader will get to know Patricia Roberts Cline by hearing her speak for herself and for many with whom she identifies passionately: feminists straddling fifty and older who worry about their young sisters' silences; female artists who seek to reform the art world's steep, male-centered hierarchies; and the physically challenged and homebound whom the mainstream sees rarely and often forgets. As one of the marginalized herself, Pat hardly expected her words to be read by strangers when, early in 1990, she started committing her thoughts to the first in a series of notebooks. Not

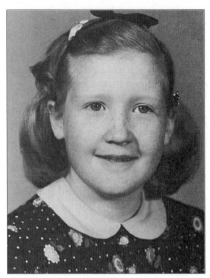

Patricia "Patsy" Roberts at age 11

public acclaim, but rather her conscience and sense of self-worth are what led her to speak in her journals for those less able to speak for themselves.

Pat's private writing goes back to 1983, when in college she dutifully filled a notebook for a class called "Women's Voices as Writers and Artists." It was there, in her journal, that she and I met, first relating as student and teacher, and then as we talked one-on-one, as sisters in spirit. Sadly, that first spiral notebook was lost, and yet it survives as the one I remember most vividly. The subject of quilting had come up while we were reading *The Color Purple,* and Pat, who always arrived out of breath and talked little in class, would rush off with her notebook to join the discussion in private. In her small, tidy hand she told me about the importance the needle arts had for her.

Pat came from a long line of seamstresses, a number of whom had made quilts. Her mother had fingers that knew so instinctively how to perform the most difficult stitches that people had said she was probably born with her tiny hand clutching a thimble. Pat herself had just joined a beginning quilters' class as an antidote to the stresses of being in college full-time at age forty. Several evenings a week, she was learning the basic stitches by making large blocks in a range of traditional patterns, and these she would use in a large sampler quilt she was making her mother for Christmas. I was captivated, in part because, as I wrote by the entry, some of my own family's older women had quilted or done other needlework, and I had been hoping to learn more about the methods they used. This exchange quickly opened a door between us, and for the rest of the term, the give-and-take of Pat's entries and my responses to them in the margins taught me not only the difference between a pieced top and a quilt, but how naturally the ground between student and teacher could be leveled, and how it was that our paths had happened to cross at this time.

Born in Memphis, a low-lying river town in the southwest corner of Tennessee, on May 14, 1943—my student was just two years younger than I—Patricia Ellen Roberts was the first child and oldest daughter of Mary Margaret "Bea" Burke and Richard Harville Roberts. Theirs was the generation of newly married couples just starting families and getting to know them when World War II broke out. Patsy's father, a young man of high ideals and poetic feelings, had put aside his early dreams of becoming an artist in deference to his parents' wish that he become a physician. When he got the word that he was a first-time father, he was already stationed in Pennsylvania with the Medical Corps, and was able to see his daughter only a few times before being shipped overseas. At the war's end, he came home "a stranger to strangers," as Pat put it fifty years later, still smarting from tensions between them and grieving over the loss of the father who sent her long letters conveying his love when she was still too young to read.

When Patsy was in the fifth grade, her father decided to move the family some two hundred miles to the south and set up a small-town practice in Houston, Mississippi. By this time his first daughter's talent for art had become apparent, as had a chronic disease that had already slowed her down more than once but would also serve as the catalyst for her talent's development later in life. Even before "the bad cold that never did go away" was diagnosed as cystic fibrosis, doctors predicted the girl would not live to be older than twelve. And yet, outliving this grim prognosis and its revisions, Patsy Roberts was able not only to graduate with her high school class, but also to go on to college. It was during her first semester at

Patsy with her parents, 1943

what was then Memphis State University that her physical problems derailed her. A bout with pneumonia forced her to drop out of school and left her confused and angry. With little sense of direction, she entered a long, bleak decade of "bad decisions and wasted years" marked by impulsive marriages, divorces, business school, unchallenging clerical jobs, and a steady decline in her health that eventually pulled her out of the workforce permanently. Then marriage to Edward Cline, a veteran of the Vietnam War, and a second attempt at college, this time with a major in art, turned her life around, as she put it, at the age of thirty-seven. Two and a half years later, Patricia R. Cline turned up in my class, and by the time the semester was over, we knew our friendship was only beginning.

For one thing, we had agreed upon an exchange of creative work. I was to give her a book I had written, a biography of a gifted but unsung and long-forgotten woman artist, Kate Freeman Clark, who was born in Mississippi not too far from where Pat had grown up. She, in turn, would make me a quilt for my office wall, to celebrate and preserve the memory of the course where she had begun to find her voice as a woman writer and artist. About a year later, when she came by my office to give me the quilt and happened to mention that she had done most of the close handiwork in the hospital, I got my first glimpse of how she was having to straddle the worlds of sickness and health, dividing her time between weeks of treatment to keep chronic lung infections at bay and her business on the outside as a student, artist, and wife. As it hung in my office, the delicate piecework, on which she had stitched all her classmates' names, not only kept this class fresh in my memory, but reminded me every so often to check in with her. "I'll bet you're just calling to see if I'm still alive," she would greet me playfully, and I, only half joking, too, would admit she was right.

Pat received her B.F.A. magna cum laude in 1987, and while her life's physical boundaries were being pulled in as her health grew worse, she was stretching the limits of what she was able to do with fabric and thread. Her relationship to her quilting had changed since that day she had joined a beginners' class to relax. It was not just that she had discovered her natural aptitude for the needle techniques and had taken to drafting her own designs, amassing a fearless repertoire of patterns and winning acclaim in regional shows. More essentially, she had ceased to consider her work with cloth as recreation. She was using it now as a serious vehicle for artistic expression and a way to embody the tensions in life and the essence of cherished relationships.

This shift was accelerated by her problem with fumes from thinners and solvents that hovered about in the painting and printmaking studios in college. But even before these pollutants became too much for her lungs, she had come to believe that fabric and thread could achieve the highest expressive significance if she handled them in the same way she had used oils on canvas, and so she had turned to her needlework for a safer and friendlier medium. "Like a painter," she now would explain, "I do not compose in one continuous line, but work in different parts of the design to bring out dimensions of objects and movement, qualities that give the quilt more than a flat, static surface."

Pat was well aware of her heresy in making such claims for a medium the art world had long dismissed as a lowly craft. But she was prepared to stitch with a vengeance to prove the authorities wrong. "Sometimes I work until 3 a.m. and start working again upon waking without even stopping to comb my hair," she would boast

11

in her journal after a marathon, pointing to the results with uncon-
cealed pride. "My works are soft, but they are stronger than any
canvas I ever painted." Constantly testing the limits of what her
materials could convey, she was mastering different techniques with
each new construction: stained glass, appliqué, intricate piecing, and
silk painting.

In January 1990, Pat made an effort to come back to school,
signing up for one of my graduate classes in women's literature.
Her physical problems had taken a turn for the worse, and she
hoped some new course work would lift her spirits and give her a
new surge of energy. Unwilling to scuttle these plans even after she
found herself back in the hospital hooked up to an IV that kept her
on antibiotics day and night, she wrangled permission to check herself out for several hours two evenings a week. She would enter
our classroom still wearing her patient's identification bracelet, a
strip of pink plastic, reminding us, like a badge of honor, that she still
refused to be taken captive by chronic illness without a good fight.
But for all her determination, the effort to walk the short distance
from the parking lot and the cigarette smoke in the buildings won
out, and after a month or so, she had to withdraw from the course.

If this disappointment felt like defeat, it quickly became the catalyst for another triumph, challenging Pat to take stock of her own
resources and what she could accomplish away from our campus.
Providentially, just as I learned that she had had to drop out of
school, I heard that some friends were planning a women's bookstore in midtown Memphis. They were going to call it Meristem,
after the botanists' word for the memory cells that remind a plant's
different parts—its blossoms, leaves, roots, and stems—that they
have emerged from a common seed and are part of a single plant.
Meristem's owners intended to showcase the books and talents of
women. So Pat was able to be first in line with a one-woman show
of her art. With the help of her family and friends, she completed a
sizable body of work, "Connecting Threads," in time for the March

Alice Walker and Pat's Enlightenment *quilt at Meristem Bookstore, April 1991*

1991 opening. By a stroke of poetic justice that brought her the ultimate reward, the quilted pieces were on display when Alice Walker came to the store to sign books, allowing the artist the rare satisfaction of knowing her work had been seen and touched by one of the muses who had helped to inspire it.

The first of the journals from which this collection of Pat's private writings was drawn was the one she began for the women's literature course in January 1990. Except for its bright pink cover, this spiral-bound, 8 ½" × 11" notebook was twin to the one she had kept for our first course together seven years earlier. Like its predecessor's, this journal's agenda was largely autobiography. It related what we had been reading in class to the student's experiences, often burrowing back to the past to retrieve some illustrative memory, or serving as drawing boards for the author's dreams for the future, and always providing a safe place where she could speak freely. Never merely a class assignment for Pat, this notebook became a companion on which she depended increasingly. Her entries not only reflected the troubled waters, but helped to quiet them as she tried to navigate through her strange double life. They steadied her feeling of drift when she was alone in the hospital with an IV, and they stilled her agitation when she drove to campus and then tried to walk from her parking space to the classroom. By the time she had to stop coming to class, she was too attached to her journaling to give it up, too. When she filled her notebook, she started another, and then she tried to keep several going simultaneously: one for personal miscellany, another for spiritual or religious reflection, and several others for quilting and art.

The quilter in Pat was hardly surprised when this impulse to put thoughts in separate compartments was blocked by her mind's better sense of its own complexity and the need to let its impressions associate freely. Her sewing and journaling, after all, were kindred acts, by nature ambitious for wholeness and change and diversity. Both dramatize the interplay among earthly struggle, spiritual striving, and artistic creation. Pat's journals, quiltlike themselves, are a wonderfully customized stage for a life that is fluid, always in progress, ever gathering up new threads and pulling together layers of meaning.

These journals give Pat a generous work space, a studio annex with room to consider the seemingly endless potential of her fabrics and to detail the process of transforming them into art. (A great mass of technical notes would have to be sifted out and distilled for a studio talk at the end of this book.) Of the well over four hundred pages, in eleven notebooks, she used roughly one out of every four to write about her cloth constructions. Exhaustively she explained her techniques—the appliqués, "stain-glass," "cathedral windows," "prairie points," mitered corners—and noted her fabrics and threads, their textures and colors, and how they were dyed. She gave vital statistics, rates of growth, and accounts of special developments: a grueling "charm quilt" takes her "forever" but makes her feel she can survive anything; an application of paint looks awful and has to be chipped away with a needle; a subtle adjustment of color at the last minute transforms a quilt she has worked on for years. Other entries relate conceptual matters, sometimes reconstructing the circumstances that led to a project, sometimes describing how research and reading enriched her symbolic content. And throughout, her pages also serve as a handy drawing board where she can experiment with designs, sketch out grids, and make her record more graphic.

The running account of Pat's studio work opens onto a larger scene, enlivened by a patchwork procession of colorful characters. Her numerous and endearing relatives, emissaries from four generations, bob in and out, bringing with them new strands to stitch into the family story. Though their lives keep them busy and scattered, they never fail to appear when she needs them. These kinfolk of hers—her grandparents, uncles and aunts, siblings, nieces and nephews, and always above all, her mother and her husband, Eddie—give down-to-earth meaning to lofty phrases about family values and loyalty.

Making briefer appearances here are the nuns from St. Anne's, their robes in the 1940s and 1950s enveloping them in mystery as they teach Patsy's vintage of six-year-olds their catechism for First Communion. Later, a business school teacher of Pat's, in heavy braces following polio, prepares her student to champion those who dare to be "more than defective bodies." From time to time, we see college classmates, hospital patients, and medical staff whose buoyant and sometimes eccentric spirit helps Pat to survive the demoralizing ordeals of institutional care. Here, too, are the rich and famous: the movie stars, athletes, artists, politicians, and pundits who visit with Pat on her TV screen. Yet it is the lesser lights who achieve the most memorable celebrity, thanks to Pat's sharp eye for small moments of glory: a hospice nurse, a whiz with IVs, roars in on his motorcycle; neighborhood children bring her their drawings and poetry.

But however entertaining the visits with her on the good days, however delightful her aptitude for exposing absurdities with a wry humor, her ultimate motive for writing about her world is prophetic. At heart, she wants to transform other people by bringing them her perspective, by helping them see how different things look to people confined to the outskirts. This, she believes, is why she finds herself writing as if to relative strangers, why she feels obliged to explain, for instance, that Eddie is her husband who works on Saturdays, even with no conscious expectation that somebody else will read what she writes. As Pat's physical space grows narrower and her spirit rebels against being closed in, her memory and imagination expand our boundaries by taking us into some neighborhoods of experience rarely visited by people who are healthy and mobile.

By putting us in Pat's position and shifting our center of gravity, the journals change how we see reality. From her vantage point, it is active people who live on the outskirts of life, and she who lives at the hub. Theirs is the "out there," hers the "right here," and the tension between them is felt in almost everything she writes. "I have these two images of myself," she tells me in 1995. "First, I am this pathetic, very sick person who is alive beyond usefulness in a health-conscious society, so people do not want to 'see' me." They want "to look away," and their fear is palpable. But she longs to be seen as the woman she is, as "a human being with the same frustrations and joys that anyone has," as someone "affected by politics, family events, and a small dog who worships" her. Through this lens, "you might see your daughter, or sister, or mother," and "so you are not afraid."

Pat's entries frequently show her trying to bridge these reality zones to make sure others know she is not the feared stereotype. She is "not a pariah," she tells an insurance review board, though she has been treated like one. She is a concerned and responsible citizen, one who bothers to vote by absentee ballot even when "so many suits and so much nonsense" in politics limit her choices. She contributes her share of community service by working at home late at night taking calls for a crisis hot line. In addition, she has a vocation and takes it so seriously that most days she dresses as if going out to a studio, though in truth, she works on her art in a bed in her den with an oxygen tank nearby. No, she is not idly waiting around to die, she tells the powers out there. She needs to be seen and respected for who she is, she insists, not because she stands out as "a somebody" but because, she declares, she is all of us.

The powers Pat writes to in protest can probably never appreciate, as we can here, how much she must overcome to take a public stand or how qualified she is to speak for others as well as herself. For her letters do not reveal the familiar paradox that runs through her journals: difficult as it is to have others treat us as second class, it is often as hard to see ourselves as the persons we champion publicly, especially when our past failures and frailties seem beyond redemption. As her contacts outside of her family thin out and time seems to pass without moving, the writer has trouble enough many days just knowing that she is alive; she only assumes that she is, she says, because she can see the rows of stitches and words she is leaving behind. But her tracks show, too, that even on those best of days—when her breathing is easier and a project carries her off on a lively adventure—it is hard for her to believe she really deserves life's ease and rewards.

Pat's quilting, no mere diversion but always a serious form of creative nonfiction, documents her effort to script a life that she

Patsy, mid-1940s

can inhabit without sacrificing either the past that fills her with shame and pulls her back or her need to move forward so she can accept the gifts of a loving God. One after another, her fabric constructions unfold as attempts to embody God's gifts as they have been embodied by her relations with family and kindred spirits. Her many editions of self-reformation show her persistence in making a place for both darkness and light on a unified field, patiently stitching a path from the one to the other, moving away from a fundamental fragmentation and chaos to coherence and clarity. In this process, fabric arrangements that do not work well, bad connections that need ripping out and replacing, and fortunate failures that show the extent to which art has a mind of its own—all these natural features of quilting become metaphors for her struggle to reconcile the disparate forces in human stories.

The journals, as much as the quilts they describe, incorporate this unruliness, which makes it quite impossible to tame a real life by removing its conflicts and incongruities. Themselves a form of piecework, the journals share quilting's impulse toward unity as well as its adversarial respect for disparity. Their pages spread out a mass of narrative remnants, all parts of one story, but such an assortment of textures and shades that the author has trouble discerning a pattern or fitting them into a single design. As she watches her many selves make their way back and then forward from the past, she wonders how any one person could harbor such different and warring factions, how she could have been so disconsolate and self-destructive at certain times and at others so hopeful and fiercely creative. The temptation might be to leave something out to make the record more manageable. But Pat is unwilling to let go of either the prodigal daughter who wandered ten years in a wilderness or the older honor student, wife, artist, and talented aunt whose quiet unorthodoxy inspires her nieces. As a consequence, she is frustrated in her attempts to impose greater order by using her journals to file the fragments, the "odds and ends of notes and scraps," incoming letters, and clippings. What she sees preserved in her overstuffed books is life's chaos, not organization. Brought to a moment of truth, she concedes that she has only carried her one "disorderly life" into four or more "confused volumes."

But what Pat has also managed to do is achieve with her fabric and writing the integrity that distinguishes art from technique or virtuosity. In her journals as in her needlework, the quilter's reward for her faithfulness to a never-ending process is having a cloth that is more nearly whole, and whose range of memory offers a broader and more revealing perspective. On this fabric, the artist can see all the moments she snatched up and tried to arrest. In tandem, they reappear as motion taking on contours of growth and resilience. In short, she can read on a longer text the wisdom that comes with time's passage and age.

The artist's passion for such a labor and appetite for tackling such complex, unruly material was fed by her own disobedient nature. Her work was informed by a sympathetic rage for freedom that bucks at boundaries and patent assumptions, especially those that encroach upon her authority as an artist and woman. Even as a novice quilter, she showed a dislike for taking instructions and tried to find ways around them, creating her own designs and making up her own rules, no matter how costly. Early on she began to grapple with infamous, uncooperative fabrics and innovative techniques that seemed to defy the laws of physics. But, invariably, these risks and investments of time paid off. Always egging her further off limits, the maverick in her helped her fight the depression that stalks those with chronic illnesses and problems. It taught her the value of pushing herself, of constantly learning something new and looking in new directions, and as each successive breakthrough emboldened the artist to tackle one more, she came to define herself much more by her ability than her disability.

To the eye untrained in the needle arts, the quilter's resistance to limits is easier seen in her journals, where each new entry readjusts the narrative boundaries to fit a life that keeps getting longer despite all expectations. Marked by the same creative misbehavior we see in her quilts, these notebooks—where Pat liked to start writing on the last page—challenge the narrow perceptions that stunt people's growth and divide their communities. Low-keyed and couched in sly humor, her observations target elitists and those in powerful places whose outlooks diminish the stature and rightful authority of less fortunate folks. She quarrels with those who look with disdain from their perches high in the art world as if her cohort of quilters were merely hobbyists or in therapy. She questions the professionals whose regimented advice for lost souls makes but few allowances for the untidy suffering people actually have to contend with. She also turns a prophetic eye to the narrow perspective of younger people whose fast-forward mind-set leaves them painfully ignorant of the past and bereft of its legacy of traditional values. As an older student returning to school, she winces when she sees how her classmates' lack of this grounding deprives them of discernment and sympathy in matters of race, class, and gender.

The last of these serious blind spots is the one that draws the most passion from Pat, whose feminist sensibilities, aroused by her first journal years ago, continue to be a driving force. There is nothing more pressing, she says in her entries, than trying to make the world better for women. She means to enlarge women's place by revising society's androcentric descriptions of truth and skewed perceptions of God-given roles. However unnoticed her contribution, however distant her audience, she vows to do all in her power to add to the record of what women know to be real: what they feel as the occupants of female bodies, what they think and observe, and what they contribute when freed from the cramped quarters of tradition. "If the flap of a butterfly's wing can change weather a hundred miles away," she declares after hearing it said by feminist Gloria Steinem, "then every woman who fights for the freedom to reach her full stature can make a difference. It is all about feminist thinking," Pat says as she works on her heavy *Victorian Echo*, a quilt created to warn the future's women about the oppressive ideals that smothered their forebears. Her *Symphony* series returns to this theme, at once cautioning women against the illusions and showing the path to emancipation. *Environmental Concerns* again exposes the fears and myths that hold women prisoners in a free society by barring them from the full range of opportunities and causing deep divisions within their ranks.

Pat's feminist impulse goes hand in hand with her quilter's understanding that beauty and strength are achieved through associations of disparate elements. As passionate for inclusion whenever she speaks about women as when she makes art, she pleads from her own experience for a more affirming way of defining ourselves as women. She would have us celebrate women's variety as well as the common threads that unite us. Pat knows her life has been richer because, however unbidden, her illness brought her the gift of intimate contact with an assortment of women—from clergy and student doctors to wheelchair runners and maids—whose ages and races and stations in life would have otherwise made them all strangers. Having kept as watchful an eye on these sisters as they kept on her through the years, she discerns that they are all kin in a common story. Her hope is that growing numbers of women, without needing sickness to serve as the leaven, might know the rewards of getting past the distrust and divisions that weaken our world. Instead of describing our female identities on the basis of what might divide us—our colors, religions, abilities, sexual preferences, ages, and occupations—Pat asks us to join her in celebrating variety as the glory of one grand piecework whose spirited threads bind us all together.

PART II:
FROM THE
JOURNALS

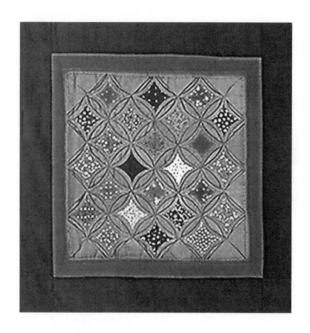

Great-grandmother Dora Gillespie with grandchildren in the 1930s. Pat's father is in the second row, seated at left.

PART II: FROM THE JOURNALS

[Pat's health had been declining rapidly for almost two years when early in 1990 she decided to take a few graduate courses at the large state university in Memphis in hopes of regaining a sense of direction and a more positive attitude. Hospitalized for treatment with antibiotics just before the semester began, she got her doctor to authorize furloughs two evenings a week so she could drive to the campus and go to class. The journal that she was required to keep for her course in women's literature—a fluorescent pink, spiral-bound notebook of 8 ½" x 11" lined sheets—inaugurated the record she kept for the next six years, the rest of her life.]

24 January 1990

As I drove back here from my class tonight, I felt grateful for the chance to escape this suffocating tiny room that is my three-hundred-dollar-a-day space in the same hospital where I was born in 1943. It was such a relief to have my thoughts pulled, if only temporarily, away from a world of introspection: How do I feel? How many cc's of urine this hour? How long has the needle been in? Sometimes, to avoid more pain, I fib when I answer, like a child. A year ago, I swore I would not come back to the hospital. Two weeks ago, I came back because I realized that my death, like my life, was not going to be a simple thing. It was the limbo between the two I couldn't tolerate, and I still had a choice of one thing or the other.

I've read somewhere that women tend to associate their grandmothers with some ideal expression of womanhood. I believe it because it is true in my case. I was born during World War II, when

Pat's maternal grandmother,
Catherine Joanna Horan Burke

my mother was living in her mother's house, along with her father and younger brother, while my father was overseas in the army. I'm sure the crowded conditions sometimes made things tense, but all I vaguely remember about my first years is my grandmother's gentleness, her perfume, her way of singing me to sleep with Latin hymns, and how much she loved me, a fact I never questioned as long as she lived. I spent weekends at my grandparents' house until I was ten, and frequently, when I was ill, my grandmother stayed with me at our house.

So far, the only book on our class reading list that I have been able to get is Toni Morrison's *The Bluest Eye*, but in its first pages I read words that convey feelings from my own childhood memories: "I do not know that [my mother] is not angry at me, but at my sickness. I believe she despises my weakness for letting the sickness 'take holt.' " By the time I am ten, there are three other children, my father has decided to move to Mississippi to practice medicine, and there my parents are involved in a daily therapeutic routine with me, as parents of children with cystic fibrosis are.

25 January 1990

I am waiting to hear if I will be discharged tomorrow or will spend another week here. I am feeling better and want and need to go home. My husband bought this "hot pink" notebook-journal for me while I was in class last night. He hands it to me in a plastic bag with the Memphis State tiger on it. He had slipped in some gowns and underwear for another few days, "just in case." I tell him how grateful I am for him. He says he's grateful he didn't run any lights and get stopped and searched!

I'll get out in time for tomorrow night's class.

28 January 1990

For almost forty-seven years now, my life has fluctuated back and forth between a struggle to survive and, surviving, a struggle to live as normally as possible. There have always been so many things I wanted to do, and I have been fortunate—no, I have been persistent—and managed to do most of what I really wanted to do.

My journal should improve as my life settles back to normal. I have stacks of scribblings I've been unable to organize and insert.

29 January 1990

One day a couple of years ago, I was overwhelmed by how fine a line I had walked between a fight to stay alive and a wish somehow to be able to die quickly and peacefully. Contrary to what I said in the '50s to the nun who taught me in the fifth grade—"Yes, Sister, I would be willing to die for my faith"—deep down, I knew I wouldn't. I hoped I would never be tested. I knew I could never take my own life. I still am not sure if I am a coward or a rational human being.

I volunteered two years ago at the Suicide and Crisis Intervention Center. At the in-service training sessions, psychologists from the University of Tennessee often discuss at great length and with clinical precision the different types of depression, degrees of lethality, psychotherapeutics, and so forth. But there is a soft-spoken

Indian doctor who always takes a different tack. I remember his first words to us: "If you think you are here to save someone, to be heroic, you probably won't like it. Most of the time, the callers won't hear what you say. But, if you listen and hear what they are saying, you will learn more about yourself, and human nature, and other people than you could ever learn in any other way." (This reminded me of something Karl Menninger said at age eighty-seven: "People have been talking to each other for thousands of years. How did it come to be worth $60 an hour?")

So we're "listeners" for people who can't afford therapists and are often so ill and adrift—as they bounce from jails to psychiatric hospitals, which quickly release them because of a lack of space—that we seem to be the only people who care. There are a lot of regular callers. Recently one of them, a young woman who is severely disturbed and usually hysterical and shouting expletives, called at 3 a.m. This time her tone was completely subdued; she was breathing heavily into the phone. I discovered that she was sedated and had been arrested some hours before—probably for causing a public disturbance—then transferred to the Crisis Stabilization Unit and tranquilized, then taken to an apartment of some kind, with a mattress and a phone. "Temporary deinstitutionalization." At first she rambled on about "stun guns" and "cops"; then she made the most rational statement I have ever heard her make: "Lord, Lord, Lord, I'm never in my life going to have what I want." When I asked her if she could tell me what she wanted, she slowly began a list most women would easily understand: "I want a house, with curtains on the windows—I want my kids back (she lost custody of three children long ago)—I want to be thin—I want a man to love me—I want to get my stuff out of storage, but I've lost the key now; anyway it's just old junk, but my kids' pictures are there—I just want my momma back."

She never said she wanted to be well because she doesn't know she isn't. For a tranquil few moments of her life, she shared what my life could have been if my mind, instead of my lungs, had somehow been damaged at birth.

11 February 1990

Sunday is sometimes a troubling day for me now, as I feel more and more that I need some spiritual source to draw strength from. My memories are bound up in the mystical Catholicism of my childhood, but it's been almost thirty years since I left the church as an angry young woman. Now when I go to the First Communion of a nephew or niece, I'm reminded that the church I grew up in no longer exists as it was.

When doctors here sent me to Mayo Clinic a while back, my mother's brother and his wife drove to Minneapolis to be with us. Early in the week we all ate at a Chinese restaurant—my fortune cookie said, "You will live a long life"—and after the final scans and diagnosis, much better than expected, my aunt and uncle, my husband and I decided to spend the next two days sight-seeing in the area. Saturday evening my uncle asked if we would mind going to mass the next day. In the old church a flood of memories came back, and so did my early connection to this sixty-five-year-old man, who was a teenager living in the house my mother and I lived in as World War II progressed. I was named after him, which made sense.

As recently as this past Christmas, he told me that St. Anne's has started having the old Latin mass again. I know he is trying to offer me something—an opportunity, I suppose, to "return"—but I am still too angry to, even now. And I know that he—as a male, a proud graduate of Notre Dame, a "Fighting Irish" football player, and a retired engineer—cannot know where my anger comes from.

12 February 1990

A few years ago I went to the funeral of Lovie Robinson. Terrified in her later years that someone would break in and harm her, she refused to leave her home even to see a doctor and died

Uncle and godfather Patrick Burke, 1943

barricaded in her old house on Alma Street. A neighbor who started to worry after not seeing her for two or three days got the police to force their way in, and there they found her, a casualty of her own terror.

Before this funeral I had recently seen *The Color Purple*, and the movie was on my mind as I stood in that old "black" cemetery. Until the movie, it hadn't occurred to me that there were separate cemeteries for blacks and whites, and little wonder, since Lovie was the first black person to die whom I truly cared about or even knew very well. Her life was as interwoven with mine as most of my relatives' lives have been. She had come to work for my grandmother when she was twelve and my grandmother was probably not much older. She was there when my grandmother died. I probably went to her funeral for my grandmother's sake, but I also felt I was letting go of someone very important to me, someone whose life should never have been so difficult in her final years.

I remember in my grandparents' blue-collar neighborhood, everyone had a "maid." My husband said this was true when he was growing up in Nashville also. I never thought of Lovie as an employee (which she wasn't to me), nor did my grandmother after a while. I don't know when the relationship changed between these two women, but probably it developed into friendship as the "significant others" in their lives had less and less time for them, or disappeared altogether. In their old age they spent many hours together. They shared many losses and loves, I suspect. They only lived blocks apart. I'm not grateful for the system that so exploited black women, and men, that many of them had two households to look after; but I am grateful for those I grew close to because they cared for me as if they had enough love to share with more than one family. I would never be one to say that such friendships as theirs were common, or that theirs in any way balanced out the racism and bigotry that existed and still exist, but they seem all the more to be valued and remembered for having existed at all.

15 February 1990

Last night's class, where we discussed Charlotte Perkins Gilman's "The Yellow Wallpaper," brought home to me that some of my own quiet panic or hysteria now is about losing ground and losing control. Often now, I find myself looking back, rewinding the reels and reliving what is behind me. If my past was not always pleasant, at least I know what it was. The future is more uncertain and disturbing to contemplate.

I always prepare to write in this journal by looking at my old photos, where I seem to be forever looking down, never up. There I am a thousand light-years ago—and my parents—standing anxiously on the small lawn of an early Memphis suburb. It belongs to the decaying inner city now. Sometimes we go by there, and I have an impulse to go up and knock on the door and ask to sit on the porch a while, but I know better.

Back then the houses were similar, like the houses today in my own suburb miles away, but the families themselves were very diverse. My mother's was Irish, her parents were immigrants; next door and across the street were Italians, Greeks, and Jews. I don't remember any other people as lightly skinned as we were; and when I was old enough to notice, it fascinated me that often the old folks spoke one language and the younger folks another. Everyone seemed to yell at each other, and there was a lot of spontaneous slapping. With the porches and open windows, it was impossible not to share the problems that too many people in too small a space precipitated. But my own memories there are good ones.

I often wonder if something wasn't lost as these blue-collar families moved away from their ethnic identity and became more like one another as they sought to become more Americanized Americans. I have nieces and nephews who are Irish, English, German, Dutch, Native American Indian, and Scottish. In Laura Ashley dresses and seventy-eight-dollar tennis shoes (not at the same time), they look and act pretty much alike, but I wonder what their dreams and their expectations are. If I felt confused being two generations away from my roots, I wonder how they must feel at their greater remove. Add divorce, and the alienation must be complete.

20 February 1990

A close friend and I often go to see movies together to escape. Occasionally, we also embark on what I call "Looking for Godot." I defer to her wishes about where to look because she has a child who she feels needs a church. (My friend never went to church herself before she became a mother; her mother was a divorced Catholic. Instead, she's been in therapy for years and years.) Once, with the little girl in tow, we went to a church where we were received—or not received—as though we were invisible. We wandered around until my friend literally grabbed someone and said we were new and asked where the services were going to be held. The woman fired back, "We don't have a singles group for women. We have a family group, a children's group, and a group for single men." We ended up being deposited in the single men's group instead of the families' group, which seemed strange. Apparently, they either thought we were lesbians and a danger to families or thought we were looking for men (as opposed to solace).

There is a line in *Alice in Wonderland* where the Mad Hatter, I believe, says, "This is an experience I shall never forget." "Yes you will," the Red Queen replies, "if you don't make a note of it." And so I am *noting* my "failure to find Godot" one rainy Sunday morning.

22 February 1990

I believe I know something about my great-grandparents today that I didn't know yesterday. A woman who just moved here from New Orleans was talking to me, in that wonderful dialect "natives" have, about the city she'd lived in all of her life. We plan to go there during Spring Break and so she was telling me about the St. Patrick's Day parade. "You gotta go across Canal, because that's where all the Irish and Italian immigrants settled. They wasn't nothing, as far as the French were concerned, so they weren't allowed in the Quarter, and they built everything too. They're still mostly there, the Irish and Italians, the ones that didn't leave." It would seem my great-grandparents, who came to this country from Ireland to escape the potato famine, weren't too crazy about digging ditches for the canals in New Orleans and settled instead in Memphis, where their offspring became firemen and policemen. This year relatives partying on Beale Street found our great-grandfathers' names on bricks preserved from a time when Memphis was a small river town.

23 February 1990

I am having a lot of trouble with this journal because I am having a lot of trouble with my life, which sometimes feels like a daily attempt at nonlife. Sometimes I try to calm myself with future plans and my quilting, which I use in place of prayer. Whom would I pray to and what would I pray for?

There have been some amazing global events recently: the Tiananmen Square massacre, the release of Mandela, the Wall coming down between East and West Berlin, "peace" with Russia. And I myself have bought *50 Simple Things You Can Do to Save the Earth*, quite a heady project for someone who has problems putting her shoes on, some mornings.

Pat's maternal great-grandfather, Patrick Edward Horan (1855–1926), Chief of Detectives, Memphis Police Department

Recently in a meeting for Crisis Center volunteers, Dr. K. again talked about how we can get to know ourselves better by listening to others. In a soft-spoken, Middle-Eastern accent, he trails off in many directions, speaking of Poe and Shakespeare and mythology, the Big Bang theory, the universe, and people living too fast. A man asks him, "What's all this stuff about women burning out?" And (not missing a beat) K. says it's about men not being brought up or taught to help in the home. Then he goes on to talk about work—any work, but especially creative work—being the most important thing in people's lives. As this gentle psychologist spins out ideas in this Southern Baptist city, I think we are being instructed by a guru—until my husband tells me the man beside him has just whispered, "What in the he__ is he talking about?"

Soon I can wear sandals again and my feet will be better. There is nothing that can be done about them; it's part of the disease process. I am fortunate; it could have happened sooner, but why don't I feel fortunate?

[Almost all people with cystic fibrosis eventually experience a phenomenon called clubbing, an enlargement of the tips of their fingers and toes that makes it painful for them to wear regular shoes.]

The other night I had a class at some distance from where I was parked, and it would be hard to say which overwhelmed me the most when I got there and could sit down: my throbbing toes or my labored breathing. The teacher was talking. It seems the subject is rape. Then a young male student says, "I know I am going to get in trouble for saying this, but it is what I feel." "Okay," the teacher says, "say what you think." He says, "I don't believe a man can really rape a woman unless she lets him." The deafening silence that followed reminded me of another class I once had where the teacher— probably wanting to illustrate that some things cannot be justified— asked if anyone could think of something redeeming to say about Hitler. Four people raised their hands. When this happened, the teacher looked stunned and said this was "a first," and he hoped it wasn't a sign of the times. But the same thing happened again the other night.

After a long pause, the teacher said, "What do you other men think about this?" Dead silence. Then finally one of them asked, "What about eighty-year-old women?" The first speaker, pulling back just a little, said children up to the age of twelve and eighty-year-old women *could* be raped, but not the average woman today. The women, of course, spoke up.

Martin Luther King, Jr., in the movie *Driving Miss Daisy*, is heard to say that what he fears most is not the hatred of "the children of darkness" but the "apathy of the children of light." I felt the same way by the end of the class.

Why can't I stay home, with my feet propped up, and watch *Wheel of Fortune*? What forces me to keep searching for clues in my own game of life, hoping to be enlightened, but often being amazed and disappointed? Will more men in the younger generation be any more helpful and aware than many men were in the past? Will they be more supportive than men who today wonder why women are always talking about stress and being burned out? Or will they believe, as I once did, that it isn't the men who are at fault, but the women? It seems to me now the whole system is to blame, the culture we're born into. It only changes slowly, and only when many of the right forces are at work.

Recently in the hospital a physical therapist asked if I had kids and thought it was too bad that I don't. "They would be so much help to you, and honey, they could do your percussion." Try as I might, I cannot imagine having my children pounding my back and locking them into this struggle that is my life. Or the pain I would feel if a young daughter with dreams of her own was driven to say, "I cannot stand this anymore; I am worn out with it." I am worn out with it too, but I can stand it myself, for there is no other choice.

25 February 1990

I feel uneasy bringing up anything feminist around my nieces, unless they bring it up, because my sisters are either opposed or ambivalent when it comes to these things. It is hard to love and care about people and know they feel the same way about you, and yet be unable to share your beliefs that a better world is possible only if males and females have equal voice and influence.

> [A letter Pat wrote me on March 25, 1990, bore the sad news that she was having to withdraw from the university. She had had to go back to the hospital early in March, just a month after having been there for a two-week stretch. By the time she was home again, she had decided that school would no longer be possible. Since the university had not yet put in place adequate nonsmoking policies, she had little choice but to stay away from the campus.]

27 April–6 May 1990

It has been said, and I seem to have proved, that you cannot bring back an earlier moment. I have thrown away my notes. I have forgotten what I felt or thought these past two months. My last notes stopped before my hospitalization in March; these begin while I am hospitalized in April. I feel very sick and depressed, and something perverse in me wants to say this to everyone who asks me how I feel. So many times, during the week before I came in, I fought off the need to sit down on a curb, on the way to my car, or in the grocery. I know, in the knowing part of my brain, that if I sit down I will be giving up. But the feeling, emotional self in me is growing very tired and confused. I believe I am very ill.

I don't understand what makes some of us keep going and enables us to keep getting up, while others die so easily. And I'm not sure who's more fortunate.

I suppose I thought that by this time I would be able to look back and see a pattern or a design. In some childish way I believed I would know the purpose of my life. There is so much about long illnesses that most people don't know, and maybe don't need to know, but I am beginning to feel that a life is no longer a life when you cannot be distracted from the sickness, when reading, or music, or even a friend can no longer pull you away from it. When you have *become* the sickness and the struggle, and it gets more difficult to remember *who* you were. When even your looking at old photos no longer works.

There is an old man, a very old man, across the hall. A nurse says he's ninety-five. He has a strong, loud voice. It is easy to imagine a person who is used to giving orders; I would have believed him less than fifty. For days he was incoherent. Gradually he began to say, "NO ... NO ... NO ... NO. Don't do that ... Leave me alone." Yesterday he said, over and over, "What are we going to do, sugar? What's going to happen, sweetheart?" Today he is saying, "Help."

The doors stay open because you have to pull them hard to keep them shut. The people on the other side are too busy to take time for this. We on this side are too sick to get up and shut them. I really don't care; it lessens the sense of isolation. And so the old man and I share our despair; we become "combat buddies" as strangers do in wartime. But he is unaware of me.

The old man is nude, with tubes and bags; he stays uncovered.

All he really has left is his deep, strong voice. No one visits him. Perhaps he was in a nursing home. I have to wonder what a mind goes through at eighty or ninety when it is transferred from one institution to another.

In the process of keeping the body alive, does the soul, or spirit, somehow get lost? Sometimes I believe that prisoners executed by lethal injection may be experiencing the most humane deaths in this country—and yet, I've come here of my own, desperate free choice. It's called "making an informed choice," as if it were possible to be informed about the future course of an illness, any more than the sharing of lives in a marriage or any relationship. The truth is that each is unique and a mystery.

7 May 1990

I am here in the hospital for the eleventh day. I began this the 27th and could not concentrate. I sometimes feel like I've had a thousand cups of coffee. They are trying to open my airways more, and it's hard to think about anything else. The air is out there, I am engulfed in it, and yet it's more and more difficult for my lungs to take it in. So, here I am. I was never an athlete and I never even cared for any kind of sports. (I guess that makes me un-American.) I tried to *be* interested, then tried to feign interest, but I just grew tired of it. I didn't care who won or who lost, or even who played what game. Oddly, though, I believe my survival to this point has been an athletic achievement. I have heard this from those who study my case. I always agree to let medical students talk to me and examine me, not so much because I believe they will learn something from me, but because their eyes are more hopeful. They are more excited about what they are doing. They lift my spirits.

A beautiful young Oriental female doctor-soon-to-be came in one day and asked her questions so gently and quietly. She smiled often, and often said, "That is sooo wonderful" (when I spoke of my little dog, or when she looked at a quilt I was working on). Looking at her long dark eyelashes against her flawless skin, and given her mannerisms, it was easier to see a geisha than a woman of science. It would be so much easier on patients if medicine were a softer science. I hope she will bring something to it and not be changed by the way it is.

An older male doctor comes in to instruct the young female student doctor. He shows her various muscles and explains how I have *compensated.* "She breathes with her abdominal muscles (etc., etc., etc.). She was actually able to walk slowly to her car to come to the hospital when some people might have experienced respiratory arrest. This is because," he says, "she has adjusted down and has remained active." In other words, I won a marathon. I climbed a mountain. At this rate, I may be able to live without breathing one of these days. Pollution will no longer bother me. Will I be sought out for talk shows? I have not yet *experienced* "the agony of defeat"; it only feels that way sometimes. Neither have I won medals for an extraordinary achievement. What and where is my victory? The cup for my mantel?

The doctor points out several other "relevant" facts about skin and muscle and bone, then leaves after telling the student to have her papers turned in by noon tomorrow.

She helps me sit up and thanks me for letting her talk to me, and she asks if there is anything she can do for me. "No," I say, while I think, "Don't let the lions devour you." "You have done so well, for so long, I *know* you will be okay," she says. She pats my shoulder.

> *Let's make quilt pieces out of these messed up curtains, she*
> *say. And I run git my pattern book.* —The Color Purple

For two days and nights I listened to tapes with earphones so I couldn't hear my own labored breathing. It took me away from the pain that is not pain, but fear. A physical therapist told me that this is why lung disease is so devastating emotionally. There is no fast relief, no quick treatment—only the slow and methodical help based on tests that take time. If you're only hurting, you can be given medication for pain. But if you can't breathe, you can't have sedatives or painkillers. You're treated with words and oxygen and fluids and bronchial dilators. My mind screams, "Help me—hurry and help me!" They fan me; they pat me; they prop me straight up on a stretcher to try to ease my back muscles, which ache from the work of trying to breathe. They do all they can and prepare to resuscitate. Gradually the dilators kick in a little, and I seem to be getting more air, but it is the antibiotics that will turn me around. I have to use my mind to control my panic. I cannot afford hysteria. All of my energy must go toward calming myself and slowing my breathing as much as possible. My mind must walk slowly away from the mad, crouching dog if I'm to survive. But I've looked into the mad dog's eyes and walked away too often, now. Though no one has won so far, I sense I am losing the game.

14 May 1990

One of my sisters and her daughter came up to see me on the weekend. I cannot sleep and only doze off in short patches of time. I am constantly coughing, and they have never seen me with unwashed hair or in such a bad way emotionally. All of us cry, and my sister and I talk about how unexpected the bad times are, and how caught up we get in our own routine problems.

> In weaving life's design, as a knot appears unexpectedly in a thread, so disappointment blocks the smoothness of life. If it cannot be corrected, then it must be quietly woven into the design. Thus the finished piece can still be beautiful—though not perfect as planned. —Author Unknown

My sisters and I often talk about being perfectionists, but there is nothing like sickness to remind us of how imperfect we are. It is total and absolute loss of control. I pretend that life is so simple that

I can be ravaged by disease for years and then die without disrupting others' lives, if only I am quiet about it.

I am very angry now, for they have put an IV needle in my right wrist and I cannot do anything. I argued a bit but realized that they have to put them where they can, and now I feel childish resentment that makes the *big* anger explode at all the little problems. It's like blaming the poor cashier for the price of groceries, or the waitress for the bad food. But who can I blame, really? What genetic or environmental error made my life so different from that of the person born seconds later?

There is a notice posted on a hospital wall here announcing a meeting: "How to Live Rationally in an Irrational World." It's for the staff, but it's I who should be there.

Another one of my sisters sent me a box of little presents this week. A toy car and a note from my nephew, who last time addressed his card "PATS WHY?" for fun. In a fit of morbidity, I told my husband it's what I should put on my gravestone. My sister sends candy and two books—*The Handmaid's Tale* and *Family Pictures*—and a box of tapes with "News from Lake  Wobegon." I have felt through the years how hard she has tried to let me know that she cares about me, in spite of my being a "poster child" sister who somehow survives beyond reason. Two years ago we shared a strange experience and that has made us much closer. Both of us cried at my nephew's First Communion, something nobody cries at. Weddings, yes! Communions, no! We didn't have full-scale emotional breakdowns, but were filled by a rush of deep sadness and are still not sure where it came from. I think it had to do with beginnings and endings. This nephew was the last child in the family.

I may go home soon. It's been seventeen days. I can walk down the hall alone and without oxygen.

"*Last night the old man died. Today the room is empty.*" I wrote this here when I woke up one night and thought I heard the old man across the hall cry out. It was the night after he died, and I suppose I thought that if I wrote down that he was gone, it would be so and put the matter to rest so I would not be haunted. Still, it may be that his is one of a thousand or even a million souls that remain forever a part of the hospital after their bodies are gone. Whatever the case, the old man crossed over to the other side, and I backed away from it, almost in unison. I now have a program ahead of me to gradually build up my leg and arm muscles again. Just walking makes my legs ache as if I've done strenuous exercise, but I feel up to it now, at least today.

This week a woman walked out of her room and down the hall and then started shouting, "Praise Jesus!" She said she hadn't walked in four years, and others came out of rooms into the hallway to witness this modern-day miracle. Okay, I say to myself, why *her* room and not *mine*?

Later on, an aide who was making my bed asked if I had heard about the miracle. I said, "Yes," thinking I'd leave it at that, but he pressed on, "What do you think of it?" "Well (*I am careful*), I think that's (*I am cautious—wonderful? ridiculous? astounding?*) interesting. I know her family must be happy."

"They said she's faking to get attention, but that she really hasn't walked in four years. She has a heart problem, but now she's on the psychiatric floor." (*Eudora, Flannery, where are you?*)

What can I say? I just listen.

He goes on: "You know I want so much to believe in miracles, that God could really make something that special happen. I believed it in my heart when I saw her taking those steps; then everybody spoiled it. Sometimes I feel very discouraged here. Last week three people died on this one side."

For some strange reason I am reminded of a movie I saw once, *The Gods Must Be Crazy*, where a native in Africa, running across the plains, finds a Coke bottle and forever after his idea of "god" is complicated. I want to tell this young aide that *believing in your heart* is the miracle: *believing* instead of *not believing*, in spite of what you see every day.

Until now I have been unable to write about my husband because it hurt too much even to think about him. I feel that in drowning, I have grabbed him and am pulling him under with me. I have spoken to him about divorce—suggested, begged at times, that he not wait it out with me any longer. All he ever says is, "I love you." I have even thought of running away and leaving him in peace, but that seems wrong, too, and stupid. I know my income and insurance would take care of my physical needs, but emotionally, he is my strongest link to life. I have never told him this because I don't want him to feel I'm clinging. For seventeen years he's been there for me. The past ten have been fraught with illness, but he gets out the photo albums to remind *me* of the good times. I'm the one who forgets when I'm not feeling well.

My husband talks of being lonely at home these days. I long for the privacy there. I can hardly read a book here now that I am doing better. Someone is constantly in and out; I even get treatments all night, so I never dream, or at least don't remember dreaming. I want to be home with my husband and my fat little dog, and I am to go home very soon. There is always a small "culture shock" and a certain adjustment to make, with more space and more to think about. But I am so grateful to be looking out at the city from my fourteenth-floor window and knowing that I will be "out there" again after almost three weeks.

The doctors and therapists want to put me in the rehab unit until I am stronger and have more resistance to illness, but I cannot spend any more time away. I believe I can work myself back to better health. They are skeptical, and they may be right.

Perhaps if I go home and see that I can't pull it off, I'll go in. Today the physical therapist asked me about the rehab unit, and I told her the doctor had suggested it, but I wasn't going right now. "Suggested it?! Honey, he would have wheeled you right over there himself if he had seen that list you were working on yesterday!" (She was talking about all the things I've lined up to do when I go home.) But she understands. She's a woman, and, like me, the "organizational chairman of her domain." She's the one who's given me the name of a good cleaning service, because, she said, she did herself that favor a few years back. I'm optimistic.

17 May 1990

I have called and made an appointment to go into the pulmonary rehabilitation unit next week, but I could not have done it without this week to myself here at home. I am trying to have a more positive outlook regarding my situation.

Yesterday Jim Henson, the Muppets' creator, died of a bacterial pneumonia, or so it's reported. Last week I survived a similar infection. He was wealthy and famous. I was fortunate. We both put ourselves in jeopardy by not getting treatment quickly. I was so sick in my bedroom the last few hours before I went into the hospital that I was almost afraid to go into it when I came back home.

[In June, when Pat had filled the last page of the notebook she started for class, she sent it to me along with a letter of apology for its late arrival. She had almost not turned it in, she explained, but hated to leave the impression that she had abandoned it when she dropped out of school. For, in fact, she continued to feel that she was still a part of the class and involved in its conversations even as an unseen participant. She wanted to thank me by letting me see how faithfully she had kept her journal and how it had helped her to watch herself playing the hand her strange life had dealt her.

Her story, though really no more than "about an ordinary woman," she said, was nonetheless an ongoing series of unimagined concessions. The most recent was having to keep a supply of oxygen in her house and having to use it virtually all the time. This had been a condition of her release from the hospital and was so distressing that her hands had shaken as she signed the papers approving its delivery. At home, she argued with the delivery man when he came with the tanks and it was two days before she allowed him to bring them inside. Life seemed to be boiling down to learning to live without what she had lost and making the most of what she had left, she told me.

Her letter led me to suggest that she use this unoccupied time to assemble a one-woman show of her art. Pat's response was to start a new journal and sketch out some quilts.]

1 July 1990

This week I will begin in earnest to complete the quilt projects I have in progress and to design and complete new projects for a one-woman show sometime the first of 1991.

It will require discipline and hard work. It will require belief in a future, and belief that I have something to say worth hearing and seeing.

This winter and spring have been so difficult that I feel this may be my last chance to leave something of myself, some record of what I have felt and tried to accomplish.

Actually, I think that my willingness to try to keep learning and my desire to understand are the keys to why I have lasted so long. The more I know, the more confused I may feel; sometimes, as strange as it seems, the important thing is the sorting out process and being exposed to the ideas of others.

2 July 1990

I am almost certain that the two things in life that have caused me the most pain have also provided the impetus behind my desire to study and create. These two things have been (1) my long, long illness and the resultant depression and (2) my failure to be "the good wife," or "good woman," in any conventional sense. I do not consider myself a "bad" person; I harbor no guilt on this score. But a part of my soul refuses to play a diminished role because of my gender, just as it will not accept an identity that reduces me to my illness. This rebellious, proud part of my nature has made me desire, more than anything, to leave behind a body of work so splendid that it will block out what my physical life was like.

I am starting to work on my projects this week, beginning with the completion of my *Phoenix* wall hanging and the laying out of my

Modern Victorian Crazy Quilt. What I want to convey with the second of these is the troubling similarity between the Victorian era of 1837–1901 and the present, 1990. There is a familiar discrepancy between the Victorians' prudish, narrow-minded, surface pretense of moral purity and the reality of the record they set for venereal disease and prostitution in England. Here in the United States, where the 1980s have given rise to a "moral majority" who extol family life

Sketch of symbolic detail of a willow tree for the Victorian Echo's *fan blocks*

and call for preserving "traditional" values, there is a porno shop and "adult movie" house everywhere you turn in urban America, and drugs and alcohol, wife abuse, and the high rate of divorce are enormous and growing problems.

4 July 1990

Today we cooked outside, or Eddie did, in the incredible record heat. Friends and family came over. I hope they know how much I love them.

I remember when I went back to college, I worried about not having enough time to spend with my nieces while they were still children, and I tried to make time to be with them. But I somehow knew, even without knowing how fast my health would decline afterwards, that if I didn't

Pat and her mother at college graduation, University of Memphis, May 1987

go to school when I did, the chance would be lost forever. Everything fell into place, and college, as late as it was, did for my self-esteem something I never anticipated: it allowed me to see myself as a worthwhile human being who could accomplish and create in spite of my lifelong, unpredictable physical problems. My desire to leave behind something of myself is more important to me now. But will something tangible be more meaningful than the memory of a hug? Or a meal with friends and family in July?

9 July 1990

"This is my story; this is my song." These words, from a song that I have long since forgotten, come to mind as I start to prepare for a quilt show. I hear them as I remember an art history teacher explaining that the abstract artists sought to evoke an emotional response to their work, much the same as that evoked by a wonderful piece of music. Though produced through the juxtapositioning of lights and darks, and of color and composition, the artist's visual harmonies can be experienced as intensely as the musician's.

During my frequent hospitalizations many people from different walks of life have examined a quilt or piece I was working on as they passed in and out of my room, and told me a story about a mother or grandmother who quilted or who left them a pieced top they cherish. Some would even come back with their own projects for me to see. One woman brought a quilt top with beautiful embroidery she herself had made in graduate school and also brought some wonderful lace and tatting she had done.

If, in this age of technology, people are still strangely drawn to fine needlework, they ought to be able to hear my visual song.

18 July 1990

It has been two weeks since I have sat down with pen in hand, but I have been working hard. My *Phoenix* is all done—the planning and cutting, that is. I finally found some small feathers that will add just what it needs, and I had all the pieces spread out in the living room when my sister came to Memphis this past weekend. I believe she likes it and hope she knows how much

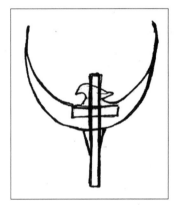

Sketch for Ascending Phoenix *with notation, "In Christianity, the Phoenix typifies Christ. Anne— healing, nurse, a good person / Christian in the truest sense / unselfish and kind."*

love has gone into my gift for her, how much she has meant to me. She "talked" me through this hospital-ridden winter and spring, and this quilt will be hers.

When I came home after three weeks, I was depressed as never before.

Something had happened to me in the hospital that had never happened before. This time I knew my lungs were going to kill me, and I was terrified. You would think I had surely known it all along and that I would be grateful for these forty-seven years and not expect more, but accepting the hard realities is not part of my nature. I had not really felt afraid until I was told upon being discharged this spring that I will have to have oxygen with me at all times from here on out, and I am no longer sure which is worse: life in my dependent condition or death.

> *A man traveling across a field encountered a tiger. He fled, the tiger after him. Coming to a precipice, he caught hold of the root of a wild vine and swung himself down over the edge. The tiger sniffed at him from above. Trembling, the man looked down to where, far below, another tiger was waiting to eat him. Only the vine sustained him. Two mice, one white and one black, little by little started to gnaw away at the vine. The man saw a luscious strawberry near him. Grasping the vine with one hand, he plucked the strawberry with the other. How sweet it tasted!* —Zen parable

Having this quilt show project is what is keeping me sane through this period. It is my "strawberry."

My *Victorian* quilt is almost all planned and well on the way. I am going to keep all my notes relating to the process itself in my quilt journal.

19 July 1990

There were difficulties growing up in our family of seven, as I suspect there were in many large families of the 1950s. I feel very fortunate to have experienced the love and affection of my maternal grandparents, especially my grandmother. She gave me her time and allowed me to be myself. In her house, in her eyes, I saw myself as special and appreciated. "You can do anything you make up your mind to do," she said, until I sometimes believed it. Whenever something meaningful has come along for me, I have wished that she were still here to share it. And then I think of the words from *I Never Sang for My Father*: "Death ends a life, but it does not end a relationship."

I wish she could have seen me in my best years, instead of my worst, though I realize I could not have survived my worst years without her love. She let me know in my twenties that I was an adult and responsible for my actions. Twenty does not know that thirty will not be as difficult, but I managed to survive anyway.

Before I stop writing today and begin working on my project, I have another issue I have been dealing with this year. I was advised to write a living will in order to achieve some control in my situation. It seemed like a good idea; however, nothing is ever simple. After reading two recent articles, I have decided to spare my husband and my doctor, and myself, this illusion of control. I will depend on them to do the best they can, as they have always done. I will do the best I can, as I have not always done.

I have no idea how I will finish all the work I have planned for my show, but I know I will. I hear my maternal grandmother whispering to me, and my paternal grandmother, who left me some tatting and crochet, pieces of which I will use in my heavy *Victorian* quilt. Both will help me. There are so many risks involved—the risk of rejection, of ridicule, of defeat—but to risk nothing is the greatest failure of all.

20 July 1990

I have completed a modern Cathedral Window quilt which I planned in a radiating mosaic pattern and titled *Sunrise Yellow Noise* (from a poem by Emily Dickinson). Almost completed are three smaller pieces: (1) appliquéd water lilies, (2) a Log Cabin variation, and (3) a stained-glass appliqué work. These more closely relate to traditional works in fabric. I have designed a phoenix that incorporates ideas I will write about later. My two larger works in process are a color spectrum piece that I spent months collecting fabric for and is finally being put together, and a modern Victorian project, which will be my most involved and risky project yet. Two smaller projects may eventually be ready in time for the show: a kaleidoscopic piece, and a color piece that incorporates black and variations of gray.

26 July 1990

I am going to the lung specialist today. I feel very sick. I am having difficulty concentrating. I feel like the Elephant Man. It is easiest to sleep sitting up with my head on the table. My life seems so uncertain, I am not even sure how I will get from the car to the doctor's office. I don't know why I am writing this, except I had the wild, weird idea that I might look at it later and get some satisfaction from knowing how much I got through. Eddie and I are working all night tonight for the Crisis Center, taking the calls here at home. Maybe that will pull me away from myself.

27 July 1990

I am not getting any better. The doctor spent more time than usual talking to me. I told him I am resigned pretty much to my situation and that I am *not* writing out a living will. If I've trusted him this far, I trust him with the finale. Probably the only two people who are aware of how sick I am and feel are Dr. Potter and Eddie, but not even they can know what my life is like now. I still have moments when I feel so grateful for the small, comforting things in my life—my little dog (who is here beside me now, with his head in my lap), my swing, or a pat from my husband.

1 August 1990

I am better. I am on antibiotics and breathing easier. The joint pain and headaches have eased up, though my feet are worse, and I am wondering if I will lose my toes before I die. I can't write any more for a while. It does me no good to write about my physical complaints. I plan to get back to my sewing.

5 August 1990

My *Phoenix* is almost finished. It is my most difficult piece in that it must all be measured exactly, and sewed exactly to fit together and form the bird on the background. I am really proud of it.

14 August 1990

I am very close to having to go to the hospital again, I'm afraid. I am so worn out. I have only been able to sleep three or four hours the past two nights.

The people who clean my house now came today. At least that is taken care of. Letting go of these tasks is so difficult, and I suspect my anxiety comes as much from my lack of control over my present circumstances as from the lack of oxygen or the lack of sleep.

But something beautiful also happened to me today that helps me forget the misery for a while. A close friend of mine called, and we were just catching up. She's having her share of problems, things like car repairs and family. When I finally told her that I may be headed for the hospital again, she casually wondered if they could do a lung transplant from a live donor, the way they do with kidneys. I sort of laughed and said I imagined it would be a little difficult to get someone to give up a lung. Then she said she would be willing to give up one lung, and one healthy one for me would be better than what I had now. It took a minute for what she was saying to hit me, and when it did, I felt overwhelmed that she would even suggest such a thing, and very lucky to have a friend who could care about me so much. I hope she knows how important she and her daughter have been to me. I try to tell them, as I have my family, so if I ever get too sick to think straight, they will know that they have made my life bearable as it would not have been without them.

Many go through what I am going through, but it *feels* like I am alone in this until, every once in a while, I realize that I have people who care, and I am not really alone. It could be much worse.

18 August 1990

Today Mother called and we talked about my best friend from years ago, who had phoned after hearing that I was sick. *Again? Still? Forty-seven years is a long time even with modern medicine.*

Of course, before the call ended, Mother cried and said she wished

I would let her come and help me, and I tried to explain why it wouldn't be a good idea: (1) You hate dogs (*I have the worst-behaved dogs that exist*). (2) My hours are erratic; I sleep when and where I can (*and you won't let me sleep with my head on the kitchen table; and you wake up EARLY and CHIPPER, so you might have time to dispose of my dogs. Just kidding*). (3) In the shape I am in, it is difficult for me to be around other people (*I feel ugly, irritable, and angry, when I am not just plain sick*). As much as I would want us to spend some time together, I do not want to hurt your feelings because of my own frustration.

1 October 1990

I stopped writing here until today. For weeks I felt as if I were getting nowhere. I worked on my quilts when I could. Writing was too painful. I divided my sleep into small segments of time so I would not get so congested. I slept at a table more than in bed; I wore headphones and played music to shut out the sound of my breathing. I did anything and everything to help myself through this. I never wanted to die, but sometimes I did not really want to live either because of the fear that tomorrow would be just like today. But then a couple of weeks ago, I began to sense some improvement. I felt less desperate about the oxygen. I began to move around more. I began to plan beyond the day and to think seriously about working diligently to finish my quilts for the show. I have thirteen or fourteen weeks left and have written out a construction plan to do what will have to be done to pull it off.

One evening during these weeks, I watched a special on PBS about "Amazing Grace," and it was as close as I have come to a spiritual experience in all of my recent illness and depression.

30 November 1990

Now the quilts are going fairly well. My show is now scheduled for March.

21 December 1990

Back in the hospital. Last night someone came into my room and remarked that I always seem so content just working on my sewing. I recently saw a movie in which someone says, "If you fear death, you will feel the devils clutching at you and tearing your life away, but if you have made peace, you will feel the angels gently lifting you up toward the light." These words reverberated in my memory for days, for now I have come to feel that I am *making peace* with my discontent. My quilts are helping me do this. They express my struggle against what has thwarted me as a woman, but also bring me comfort and a sense of continuity.

22 December 1990

Confined once more, facing a television set, attached to monitors that beep continually and keep me almost immobile, I find myself automatically "tuning in." While watching the movie *Trip to Bountiful* I learned that the line, "This is my story; this is my song" is also part of an old gospel favorite. I did not realize this when I wrote these eight words at the front of this journal. My early Catholicism and the Latin chants have faded and merged, it would seem, with my southern Protestant culture.

12 January 1991

I began my first original quilt, a coverlet in the Cathedral Window style, in 1981, the same year I went back to college. Completing this quilt and finishing college were painfully slow processes. The difference between the ages of eighteen and thirty-six was the acquired knowledge that, if I kept at it, I would eventually finish. Perseverance and having a cheerleader or two are probably more important in the long run than talent and intellect. It took me a very long time to find this out.

When I was eighteen I fell ill with pneumonia my first semester of college. I quickly became discouraged then and dropped out of school. I felt that my life was over, and in a way, it was. But now I have learned the art of patience, and whether I always apply it or not, I know that, as long as I live, if I keep "stitching" I will eventually create a quilt.

20 January 1991

When I think about it I realize that each of my quilts has a dark side. This darker background enhances color and light much more than white or a lighter fabric ever could. I feel this is true of my life.

[With less than a month before the opening of her show, Pat returned to the hospital.]

26 February 1991

Although I was unaware of it then, it was more than chance that sent me on a search for my future the same year I began to reflect on the past. It was 1981, and I was thirty-seven. I returned to college and passed a quilt shop on the way to and from classes. I began to work on an art degree and to learn to quilt at exactly the same time. The quilting alleviated some of the stress of being an older student, but little did I know how much more it would do to sustain me after my health deteriorated rapidly. My art background and quilting allowed me to put my life into my sewing.

I talk to the physical therapists as they work on me, pounding and turning and shaking me. I talked to a black therapist who stayed a while after the treatment. I told her about my quilt show coming up at the bookstore, and she talked to me about her fears that society is breaking down. She is very worried about her teenage son. I mostly listened. After she left, I began to wonder why I have never really felt separated from other women as far as race and class, and even age, are concerned. Often the hospital and rehab hospital look like nursing homes, since most heart and lung patients are elderly, and children are kept in separate wards. I have come to the conclusion that my sickness is what has kept me honest and free from any superior attitude I might have developed. (This sounds like "*I am proud to be humble.*") But my illness never allowed me to feel superior and it put me in intimate contact with women I would not have seen otherwise. I have had a watchful eye on these women who have touched me, both physically and emotionally, in these last years when I have been more an observer than a participant. And I have seen how hard life is for many of these nurses and therapists, student doctors and cleaning women, wheelchair runners and lab technicians. I sense (and some have confided) that the work is too hard with too few of them trying to get too big a job done. And for those who are raising children alone, another job starts when they get home. Yet most have taken the time with me to look at my sewing and touch it, and to ask me questions about it. They are part of why I am so grateful for the unexpected time I have had. I appreciate every moment now, especially when I feel better.

> [*Pat was released from the hospital only days before the exhibit's opening, barely in time to proof the wall texts and check the installation of the seven completed quilts and four blocks in the show. The bookstore took care of publicity and a buffet, while friends and family—arriving from Alabama, Texas, and Mississippi—gathered around the artist for her big night. It was altogether a magical experience, Pat said afterwards as she watched a short video taped by one of her sisters. In the future, whenever she felt depressed, she told me, she would watch the tape and, seeing all of her quilts together, would know that her living had "been about love more than struggle."*]

11 April 1991

I have not written in my journal since my quilt show, but recently I have started some new sketches for a quilt for my brother, Richard, and his wife, Carol, and I am trying to work out a design for an illusion quilt in a different shape. I believe it will be really

Eddie and Pat at Meristem show opening, March 8, 1991

unusual. My niece Julie and I have also gotten her quilt all worked out; it is sewn together and marked for basting. We are both very comfortable with it now.

> *[The month of April, one of the wettest on record, sent Pat in another downhill slide. She had not even had strength to go by the bookstore and pick up her quilts, she told me as May approached. She had also neglected her journals and was only now thinking of writing again. It had gotten harder for her to make entries because the words seemed to give her decline a greater authority. To get around this, she was going to try to focus instead on what she was doing creatively.*
>
> *Meanwhile, in mid-May, a few days before her forty-eighth birthday, her three sisters showed up unannounced with gifts of colorful loose-fitting dresses. Despite their conservative tastes, each had picked out*

exactly what Pat would have bought had she still been able to shop. She didn't know where she would wear her magenta and deep purple clothes, but she was certainly ready. "I just love them for ... such a hopeful gesture," she wrote. She was pleased, too, that one of her sisters had brought her another journal, this one with a short quotation at the top of each page.]

May 1991

To know how to grow old is the master work of wisdom, and one of the most difficult chapters in the great art of living.
—Henri Frederic Amiel

It seems appropriate, somehow, to keep my forty-eighth birthday cards here. I do not know how to grow old, of course, and I think it will not be something I will experience. But I have lived thirty years beyond expectations—three cystic fibrosis lifetimes—and so every day is a gift, if I can keep from forgetting. Even when I am sick there is *something* to be grateful for each day, if only my fat little pug dog, who adores me.

19 June 1991

I was looking out the window of the den this afternoon, and I was overwhelmed with how small my world has become. A fragment of poetry came to mind—I cannot remember the source or the author: "From my window the world shrinks to three leaves, one branch, and an unexpected truth ... dark and clear."

The reason I am not completely detached from the world outside is small excursions made when I feel somewhat better. Last week I got a tooth fixed. It was such a relief; I had been so afraid it would start to hurt. But it was awful at the dentist's. I would cough and then he would stop for a while. It took forever.

Yesterday my niece Julie stopped by. We talked a little about religion and God, and she said she hoped I was still keeping a journal. I said, confessing I had not been writing much lately, "When I feel bad, I just keep it to myself because I can't stand to see it in writing anymore." But as soon as I began today, I realized I missed this outlet, this place where it is okay for me to be angry with things as they are, where I do not have to pretend anything, but just maybe can come to terms with my life. And this is important because my life does go on, no matter that it is unlike anything I ever imagined.

2 July 1991

I believe I would live my life the same way if I had it to live again. Maybe in my twenties I would marry less and try to love more. But who in her youth understands anything about love? Romance or sexual pleasure, perhaps, but love came late to me. As late as my forties, actually, when I experienced it during nights of fear and sickness. When I said I was going to move into the extra bedroom to save my husband the misery of my struggle, and he said no, he felt better with me being in the same room. In a way, he has joined in the struggle and made me feel loved in my most unlovely life.

This winter as I got worse, I worried that people I care about will remember me only the way I am as I grow sicker, and I guess I wanted to die while I was something more than a burden. My greatest fear is still being seen as an illness and nothing else. I suppose everyone who is sick for a very long time feels this way, and older people who become very ill.

9 July 1991

Today I examined a truth I have kept locked up in my soul. As I was listening to a commercial promoting a tape on our most recent war—Desert Storm, they called it—I was overcome with sadness. I was overcome because I felt the pain that any war leaves in those of us who cannot, for so many years, name its source. The romance of war with the patriotic flags and yellow ribbons distracts us and keeps us from understanding. I have often wondered if others whose

Patsy with her father, Richard Roberts, 1943

fathers were away during World War II—and came home to them as strangers meeting strange children—felt as alienated as I always felt from my father and share my lingering sadness.

Last year when my husband and I went to see a replica of the Vietnam Memorial Wall and I watched him looking for names, I was given an irrevocable image of what it is to search and search for someone whom you have lost to the madness of war. From that moment last fall, I began to cry often, without being able to locate the source of the tears. This continued throughout the winter as I worked on my quilts for the show, and then the sadness stopped before the March opening. The search for its meaning and the search for my father continue, however.

10 July 1991

> *We must have the courage to allow a little disorder in our lives.* —Ben Weininger, M.D., and Henry Rabin, D.D.

How well I know about "the courage to allow disorder," for I never had this courage as an adult until recently. I believed that a neat house with straightened-out closets and tidy drawers would keep other people from seeing my glaring physical imperfections—the "cold" I caught in 1943 that somehow never quite left me—and my obvious failure at marriage in my twenties.

Though it seems so odd to me now, my immediate reaction when I was finally diagnosed as having cystic fibrosis was to straighten my home from top to bottom. I was sure I would die within five years, and who can say what inner turmoil and pain allow a human being to believe that such a display of organization will tell the greatest lie. Three sharpened pencils, a ruler, a pen, and neatly stacked note-book paper all in a row in a desk drawer say nothing. If someone had the patience to pry the drawer open now, it would be more honest. It would say of me, "I am human, and I am imperfect. I sit and visit now; I sew whenever I feel like it; I count and treasure the good moments. There is no longer a lie to tell." The truth is obvious to those who take the time to notice. For those who don't, the living room is still very neat—as it was the last time I spent time there.

12 July 1991

I love to talk to younger women. It makes me realize how old I am and how much or little life has changed. I believe they learn from us older ones what they want their lives to be like, not from what we tell them, but from what they observe about the way we live.

It is easy to become defensive and blame men, or society in general, for our mistakes. It is easy because there is a measure of justification there. What is not easy is understanding how complicated it is to change, to be what we, their models, never believed we could become. How can females in their teens, or even in their twenties, feel secure when there is so much pressure on them to conform to questionable ideals?

I had to make a terrible admission to myself this year. My own freedom from makeup and hair rinses came just this winter when I began to use oxygen full-time. These things would no longer matter when all that anyone would see was a tube in my nose draped over my ears and attached to a tank. As odd as it was, as upsetting as it was, it was liberating as well. I might have experienced this as a

Pat, April 1966

much older woman, but I experienced it at forty-seven. I feel like I did before I became self-conscious at thirteen or fourteen and quit diving for pennies at the park pool because it could ruin my hair and make my freckles worse.

12 August 1991

Today I wrote a note to the Houston, Mississippi, library about showing my quilts there in the spring. It will be the biggest risk I have taken so far, for—as they say—"you cannot go home again." I did not even go to my class reunion.

16 August 1991

Eddie's directory of those who died in Vietnam came this week. Now whenever he has some free time, he reads through the names, searching for those who disappeared in his war, the war of his youth. It makes me think of *Slaughterhouse-Five*, where Vonnegut speaks of "The Children's Crusade," of the terrible truth that children are the ones who fight the grown-ups' wars and are its needless victims.

22 August 1991

These past few days have been so good, I am *happy*. My congestion is clearer than I can remember for such a long, long time, so I have not had the anxiety I feel when I have to struggle to get enough oxygen.

I have finished the top of Julie's quilt, have made good headway on my ram's skull quilt, and have even worked on the hexagon wall hanging. It is amazing how wonderful it feels to have this break. My mind needed it more than my body did.

1 September 1991

Even though I now take care of the Crisis Center Line at home, when they switch it over to me, it still makes me feel better to be able to do something like this, when there is so much that I cannot do. It is a lucky thing for me that this particular kind of volunteer work is what I chose several years ago, when I could still leave the house. The Crisis Center newsletter recently carried an article that spoke of the "high" one can get from helping another human being. I have experienced this "high" myself, and still do.

2 September 1991

There came a point in 1991 when I realized I had crossed a line over which I could never cross back. It was extremely difficult to accept that I was in the final stage of my illness. I need oxygen twenty-four hours a day. Exertion causes swelling and a very fast heart rate. Even worse than the physical reality is the emotional and intellectual reality, and yet I do not feel ready to let go of life. There is so much I still want to do. There are moments when I know I will never walk in a park again, or go to a play or concert, and then I feel overwhelmed by the loss. I miss sharing these things with people I love, but I know I must set them free to a life without me, even though I am still here physically. From now on I will only participate in spirit.

3 September 1991

Today a very strange thing happened. Several weeks ago I had called a woman to see if she would be able to teach my little neighbor Beth. I had read about her art classes in the paper. I told her I was too sick to teach Beth myself. Today she called me back. She inquired first about whether Beth still wanted lessons; then, very haltingly, she tried to tell me about a "gift" she has, and said she would like to use it to help me. She kept repeating, "I don't want to frighten you, and I am not crazy." The gift, she says, is the power to heal. Truthfully, after talking to her for a while and finding out there was no money involved, I began to think, "Why not?"

I have been so much better the past two weeks since talking to her, it is strange. She says I have been on her mind constantly and she believes she can help me, but I must not talk about it and must realize (1) she does not know where her power comes from and (2) it does not always work, but she has helped about eight other people.

And so I agreed to see her Thursday. I have a small hope, the tiniest glimmer of a maybe. Eddie is agreeable. I think he has some small hope, too. It is like we are on a raft in the middle of a shark-infested ocean, still hoping we will be rescued, while knowing the odds are against it.

5 September 1991

Persi Johnson came by at 4 p.m. and tried to heal me. She says she has a gift and who am I to reject a gift? Of course, I asked the doubting, skeptical questions: how much does this cost? Is this connected with a religion, or is it magic? But, alas, she came and placed her hand on my curving back and we sat quietly. There are no histrionics, just quiet.

Persi, this little elderly woman in tennis shoes, says she knows she has helped me. She popped in and out. "Call me in a week," she said, "and tell me how you feel." I know I am afraid that I will not feel any different, but I act optimistic. I do appreciate every single person who has wanted to help me and am grateful for every single act of kindness.

7 September 1991

I have been better for a total of three weeks now, three long, wonderful weeks. What happened? How did it happen? Why did it happen? My healer said she has had me constantly in her mind since the two weeks preceding her visit and that she saw me every day even before we had met face-to-face.

Why do such weird things happen to me, forever complicating my life? One thing I am trying now is not to be so rational. Most people, of course, would not see me this way. My feeling is that I am widely regarded as something of a "flake," but actually, I question *everything* in order to understand rationally, which is why I am confused so much of the time. Now I want to simply accept my recent good fortune, but I keep wondering how this is going to evolve. Where will it take me?

15 September 1991

Reaching beyond yourself or pulling away from the forced introspection needed to cope with serious illness often seems like the only way happiness is possible. I have been amazed this year at the silly, small things I have used to focus outward, just for minutes sometimes, and the sense of contentment or satisfaction they give me. I hold FuFu's face in my hands and talk to him, and I spend endless hours on my quilts.

I have heard it said, "Courage is grace under pressure." I don't measure up to this. When my breathing is very difficult, I feel a tremendous anxiety that anyone who is around at these times can see immediately. When I am choking and coughing, even my dogs act stressed. They pace around. No, I am not courageous under pressure.

But cool air blowing in my face as I fall asleep without struggle, or a very good meal, or Julie's sweetness, or Eddie's hug in my unloveliness brings back memories and earlier days when life was easier, and so memory is another path to happiness.

28 September 1991

This week the older relatives in my family paid me a visit. I assured them that I was up to it, and I was! Two uncles, two aunts, and one aunt-in-law came, and while they were with me, I knew who I was again. One of the uncles talked about the craft fairs they go to. He has been wood-crafting for as long as I can remember; my aunt paints the things that he makes. They have both beat cancer, and they are pictures of health and seem to have a comfortable retirement. The younger aunt and uncle, whom I see fairly regularly, are still "the kids," joking and teasing with the others. I enjoyed—no, I *loved*—this visit.

Soon after they left, quite by chance as I made a cup of coffee, I heard a hymn on TV:

> *May the footprints that we leave*
> *Inspire them to believe*
> *And the lives we live today*
> *Help them to find their way*

These words seemed to sum up the faith that has guided these wonderful relatives of mine, who go back to my very troubled years and were always right there to help me, and have surely been praying for me all these years since. I simply cannot accept the idea heard so often these days that families are the cause of the guilt people feel about their lives, as if the older generation were somehow to blame or responsible for the younger ones' choices and actions and the emotional consequences.

3 October 1991

The poet Anne Sexton wrote that suffering reduces any human being to humiliating neediness. In this twilight of my long illness, I am discovering that this is so. I cannot call friends or family and simply say, "I need to hear a voice to pull me away from myself." So, instead, I just call and chat about nothing in particular, and it serves just as well.

In trying to keep other people from knowing how needy I am, I sew, but this can add to my stress when my quilt is in the living room, my scissors in the den, and my thread in the sewing room, and I am too sick to bring them together. So every detail of my life must be carefully planned so I can manage now. When my illness overrides my ability to function, I want to let go of my worn-out life and wonder what I am still here for. My chest and all the muscles there ache from straining for oxygen. Still, I must try harder to value every minute that I have. Despair is so unproductive.

I now make myself as comfortable as I can during these bad spells. The phone is on the couch; my books are on the couch; water, Kleenex, within reach. It would look strange to anyone who might stumble in, but it makes me feel secure. My only challenge is getting to and from the bathroom. What is so amazing is that I have actually begun to feel better now. I have survived without hospitalization, and this is a minor miracle for me at this point. I take antibiotics, I drink gallons of water. Sometimes Eddie fixes me something to eat when he comes home.

Today I am finishing up some work, so I know I am better. I called Meristem Bookstore and talked to Audrey, and Eddie is taking the quilt I have made as her gift to her. I have updated my work journal and hope to be well enough to baste Julie's quilt. I have to be able to crawl around on the floor to do this.

4 October 1991

As with each of the quilts I've given away, I registered *Environmental Concerns*, my gift to Meristem, because, as another quilter once said, "If not documented in some way, your pieces of time, transposed into cloth and thread, are as fragile as the dreams they were based on."

Meristem is a feminist bookstore, and like others around the country serves the lesbian community as well as women in general and their friends. Something interesting happened as I was frantically trying to take care of final details for the opening of my show at this store. One of my nieces, a college student, phoned right before the event and told me that my exhibit was being announced in a local gay and lesbian newspaper. She had seen it on campus and was afraid I didn't know—actually, I didn't—but I really saw no cause for alarm.

I tried to explain as tactfully as I could that when I was offered a place to show my quilts and realized the lesbian connection, it only enhanced my idea of a show there. My deep feeling is that women's progress has been so slow because we divide ourselves up according to what we are not, instead of who we are: We are *not black*, or *not white*, or *not lesbian*, or *not straight*, or *not rich*, or *not poor*, or *not old*, or *not young*. The truth is, we all *are women*, and that overriding aspect of who we are is what should bring us all together. Our gender is our connecting thread.

6 October 1991

I am trying to stay out of the hospital, but yesterday I felt very bad. My closest friend came over and just sat with me. She wanted to call 911 when she first came in and saw my condition, but I felt better with her here. My struggle to breathe eased up, and as time passed, we both relaxed. She began looking at my recent quilts, which were spread around me—I am almost always working on them—and then to my surprise, she said that she wished one day I would make a quilt for her. "You've made one for everybody else," she said. I was stunned because I had never thought of doing this, and she means so much to me. She is my closest friend, but in many ways we are very different. When I think of her, I think of the outdoors; she runs and rides a bike. She is not one to fuss about how her house looks or to have art or decorative objects there.

But she wants a quilt, "something blue." As I think about the idea of a blue quilt, it somehow seems fitting because she and I have always supported and loved one another through our "blue periods." Our forties, especially, seem to have been particularly cruel—in my own case, due to failing health; in her case, due to the loss of a twenty-year career in nursing. She is fighting to reestablish herself and deal with financial chaos. It has been a painful time for us both, but eased by the fact that our friendship goes on.

I suppose most people who know my situation would think that

Meristem Bookstore owner Audrey May with Environmental Concerns *on the wall behind her*

my best friend would naturally be a nurse. The truth is that we did not establish our friendship on a nurse/patient basis. It began years ago when she was coping with a failed marriage and my health was stable. I was just *there* for her then, as I was when her daughter was born, my most cherished memory. Seeing this newborn was the first time I ever truly saw a mother's face repeated in a tiny version. It was amazing to me how much they looked alike.

She, in turn, was *there* for me when I was going to college and fighting for handicapped parking. And she was there when I finally graduated. She even got up early one fall morning and drove over to our house—her daughter was small, and she brought her with her—when I left to go to the Mayo Clinic. Now she is here again as my health declines. Always, more than almost anyone else, when I've needed love she has been available, through good and bad times. I have often wished that I could do more for her.

And so I must try to make for her a quilt that is unadorned and timeless. No frills here, but it should have strength and a bold design. Right now I am considering a traditional pattern, perhaps Roman Stripe or Amish Shadows. It will be the color that makes it one-of-a-kind. I may incorporate blue lamé and hand-dyed fabrics. I will use every piece of blue fabric I have. Maybe I will do something unusual in the border, or perhaps give it three or four borders.

10 October 1991

And so I am back in the hospital. I have managed to stay out since last February, but here I am again. Eddie brought my quilting stuff and this journal to me. I am not *very* sick, but just sick and short of breath. And this, my "second home," always awaits my return whenever I can't keep going in my other home *out there*.

The TV is covering the hearings for Clarence Thomas, the Supreme Court nominee. What strikes me about the charges of sexual harassment brought against him by a female whom he once supervised is how slowly some things change.

But I do feel things are changing, even if slowly. The first step in correcting the problem of sexual harassment is acknowledging it. These hearings may at least move people in that direction. Unfortunately, in the course of the week, the hearings have deteriorated into television at its worst, and as the questioners focused endlessly on the pornographic details, I felt sad for the people directly involved. With issues like the national debt, homelessness, and AIDS increasingly part of everyone's lives, hours and days were wasted on this to feed our basest appetites.

13 October 1991

Appropriately enough I am working on my Illusion quilt while listening to the Clarence Thomas hearings again and wondering if we will ever know the truth about him and Anita Hill.

My doctor just came in, and my IV antibiotic dripped on my book, leaving a four-page mark, which has dried to a wrinkle. It is perfect here as a memento of all the drops that have entered and moved through my veins, my blood, my life. These clear, expensive, sometimes painful drops that have enabled me to go on living while so many others have died, most of them children who never were able to reach adulthood.

16 October 1991

One thing the Thomas/Hill hearings have allowed us all to see is that the white males in suits who run this country have little understanding about the rest of us. As someone recently said, "What we all witnessed, thanks to TV, was a process run amuck."

17 October 1991

Today I am going home, so this will be the last hospital writing for now.

I was not desperately sick this time when I came to the hospital, but as I prepare to go home, I do have the sense that I have been losing a little of my life with every visit. I do not tell anyone this because it would serve no purpose. This time as I leave I feel better but very frail, as if my knees would give if I walked very far. I think how one often arrives at conclusions through very circuitous routes. What I came to see last year is that there is no way to fathom what has happened to me, or what will happen, regarding this lung disease. There is no way to comprehend the resilience that some of us have and others do not. There is simply a lot about survival that none of us ever will understand.

Last winter, as I stopped looking for absolute answers, I also began to let go of the guilt I have felt because I have somehow survived for this long, and because my survival had made me dependent on others, who pay a price.

All my life I have fought for my independence. Now I must somehow let go with relief, not with anger and guilt. It may be the most difficult thing I have had to do.

18 October 1991

In each of my quilts I have always tried to incorporate something new, like the stained-glass technique, which I used in *Flowers on the Wall*, or the appliqué, which I used in *Sisters*, or the intricate piecing in *Sunrise Yellow Noise* and *Life's Illusions*. I once read that learning something new is the best way to fight depression, and I know from my own experience that this is so. Learning pulls one's mind away from one's self and into whatever is being learned, and the value of this cannot be overstated. For fighting depression is, and has always been, the most difficult aspect of dealing with an illness that steals your life in bits and pieces.

Yesterday on TV I heard two art critics discuss some of today's most controversial art. They talked about the "performance piece" done by "the blue men with cereal," and Christo's yellow umbrellas, and the homosexual eroticism of Robert Mapplethorpe's photographs, and the "Love, Spit, Love" exhibit featuring nude couples having sex. When it came to the question of "What is art?" they agreed it can be anything that challenges previous conceptions of art, or makes us think about something in a new way, or brings about some strong emotional response. I thought of how well my quilts (and those of countless other women) fit these criteria, and yet how unlikely it is that any of these art authorities would give our productions the time of day.

25 October 1991

The only courage that matters is the kind that gets you from
one minute to the next. —Mignon McLaughlin

The courage "that gets you from one minute to the next" is what I am praying for now. Since getting out of the hospital a week ago, I feel as though I have been through hell. Day by day the lung congestion has returned, and along with it, the side effects of coming off the antibiotic. I have *had* to quit taking the medication at home because I cannot walk from the pain that it shoots through my back and down my legs. My face is covered with a red rash. I have a yeast infection. There! I have listed my complaints. I am trying to not complain out loud for Eddie's sake. It has been a long road for him, too. I want to get rid of my pain and misery here on this page and get on with my life.

Tonight I am going to clean out and reorganize my desk files. They've gotten overloaded since I began getting sicker a couple of years ago. I should be able to sit on the floor and do this. Eddie has bought some new folders for me. I am looking forward to this sorting-out process.

A part of me wants to be sure that Eddie will be able to find any papers he may need in the future if I am not around.

26 October 1991

For many years I had an entirely false conception of *love*. I was reminded of this as I was going through my desk files and ran across the fragments of what I once believed *love* to be: a letter from a man I thought I loved for many years, who went to prison; a photo and a note from a man I married before I married Eddie, and his children's photograph. I almost threw these away, but found I couldn't. Throwing them away, even after twenty or twenty-five years, would be like saying they were worthless to me, and they were not worthless. They taught me the valuable lesson of what love is not. Love is not marrying as a teenager with teenage passion. Love is not romance from a distance, or where there is no sharing of space, no seeing the other or having one's own worst self exposed, and no having to compromise to coexist. And finally, love is not marrying a ready-made family you hope will give your life meaning when you feel your own life has none. When I did not believe in myself, it was unfair of me to think I could bring anything into the lives of other people who had already experienced a lot of pain. I know now that love is not something you expect to receive from others, but do not understand or reciprocate.

In the past twenty years with Eddie there have been the inevitable disappointments, but I have begun to know what love is for the first time, especially during this sickness. I know how I feel when he comes home from work, when he helps me with a treatment, or when he comes into a hospital room. I still feel like a taker, but I know what love is now. It bears no resemblance to what I thought it was when I was young.

21 November 1991

This Thanksgiving I am going to take a risk, the risk of going on a week's trip without getting sick. We are driving to meet my sister Anne and her husband, Greg, in the Smoky Mountains. I have been better lately and able to get around more easily. It should be a nice getaway for us all.

And life, after all, is continual risk and unexpected changes. I always thought I would someday arrive at a point where I would feel safe and comfortable. I would be about sixtyish and could just let life go on by itself with no need for balancing time, orchestrating events, or worrying about other people's opinions and feelings. But now I know I will never reach that point, and I am not even sure that I want to anymore. For I am beginning to know the meaning of *living in the now*, though I wouldn't use this phrase if there were another at

Eddie and Pat at her college graduation, May 1987

hand. My niece Julie is going to ride with us, and a big spare oxygen tank.

After Thanksgiving 1991

The trip was wonderful for us both. I hardly ever get out anymore and had grown so tired of being at home all the time. Eddie drives all day delivering mail, and anyone else would probably be afraid to take me out, so I've hated to ask anybody to take me for a ride. We ate our way through the four days. Turkey and dressing and desserts. Eating has become one of my primary pleasures these days. I *refuse* to worry about it.

This Thanksgiving was one of the *best!*

5 December 1991

I am registering Mary Jo's quilt and giving it to her this week. It is the *Sisters* quilt; it is about love and connectedness. Though I did not plan this, it is done in the very colors Monet used for his famous painting of water lilies. I noticed this odd coincidence long after the quilt was done. But I think of my water lily as representing the female artists who are, and have long been, nurtured by other females. The water lily remains attached to the water, the giver of life and symbol of birth.

15 January 1992

I realized tonight, while Eddie and I were talking, that he is my anchor, the carrier and chronicler of our memories. I tend to fight memories now because they confront me with my limitations, my physical inability to return to the places we used to go. Tonight he relived our trips to New Orleans, right down to what we wore and where. My sister Anne can do this with some of our childhood; she remembers the dresses we wore. My own memories, however, are like a large box of old photographs I have kept. The scenes are confused and out of order. Sometimes the pictures of one baby are so like another's that it is difficult to know one from the next. I am grateful for Anne and Eddie, who keep me straight, and who edit my albums so all the memories they contain are happy and pleasant ones.

28 January 1992

Last night my husband and I started talking and got to reminiscing about our life with each other. We came together in a lot of pain: his was Vietnam, and my own, broken marriages and a lung disease that cast a shadow over everything else. In each other we found an acceptance that gave each of us the strength to tackle our problems, though I had a much more difficult time than he. Now, being so dependent, I wish I could have been more help to him. I hope and believe his brother and sister will be there for him when I am gone. I just want him to find the peace in his life that living with me has made impossible.

I know that there were some good times because they went into the quilt that I made for Eddie. So much of it was stitched when we took our vacations with the family children. I wonder if it would ever have been completed without those seven- and eight-hour car trips!

1 February 1992

The economy is bad, so the paper says, citing low housing sales and high rates of unemployment. But as I sit here with my $1,600-per-month oxygen, housing sales and jobs do not mean a lot to me anymore. My husband's insurance is important to me, my husband is important to me, and tonight I realized that my doctor is important to me, as well.

I have been struggling lately with the idea of the new *single* lung transplant. I never thought I would even consider such a step, but having this option presented to me does complicate things. It seems to offer another chance. But for what? As bad as I hate to admit this, I don't believe I am up to it. I am not ready to suffer the pain involved.

Even so, tonight, when I saw a movie, *Awakenings*, I thought of my doctor and realized that, thanks to our medical "partnership," I have gained sixteen years I would never have had, and because he had confidence in me, and real respect, I was able to live and not simply exist. Without this, I never would have seen myself as anything but an illness and a failure. As the neurologist said in *Awakenings*, when people get very sick, doctors can say that it is the failure of medicine, or the body wasn't able to cope anymore; but in healing, it is not the body but the human spirit that makes the difference. My doctor recognized and tapped into my human spirit as a woman who had accomplished a number of things she was very proud of and still worked hard as an artist.

But now I see twilight approaching, and I have this last choice to make. A transplant? I believe I have had an exceptional life, when I stop and think about it. Why try to bargain for more? Give the lung to someone young who has only begun to experience the wonder and joys of living.

4 February 1992

I used to go to work, drive home, feel so tired I could hardly think, and wonder why my life felt so empty. It has only been during my years with Eddie, when I've been forced to slow down, that I have been able to get more in touch with who I am. I have picked up the threads of my life, so to speak, as they are intertwined with my foremothers, the women in my family who were housewives and who, when there was time, engaged in what are now called "the needle arts."

23 February 1992

Tonight I heard the definition of "milagros." It is *miracle*. My brother, Richard, sent me some earrings last year with this word on the card, and I was never sure what it meant, though I remembered him saying the people in Mexico, where he bought them, sell a lot of religious jewelry. Tonight because the word jolted my memory, I looked for them in the chaos of my workroom and couldn't find them. It made me promise myself, once again, to clean up my workroom. I would probably find a lot of things if I did. This room is where I have all my "quilts for tomorrow," which means stacks of material: half-, fourth-, and eighth-yard pieces of every sort of cloth, unusual prints, and all kinds of dyed fabric. Books, books, books. Unusual keepsakes. And all my patterns from previous quilts to prove I did them *my way*.

I will enjoy the afternoon I spend going through this room and imagining how I will use these materials.

22 March 1992

This week I received some lovely batik fabric I ordered, and with it a catalog of other hand-dyed fabrics from Alaska. I had never been able to purchase any before, but now I have all these colors, in progressions, for the first time! I also have some fabric I dyed myself—my niece Julie and I dyed some last summer—but, physically, I could never deal with the fumes again, or stand outside and hang the array of materials that must be dried out-of-doors. These Alaskan fabrics are wonderful and open up a whole new world of possibilities.

A poem by a performance artist and fabric artist, Jane Przybysz, gets to the heart of the quilting experience when it describes batik, and her "wallowing" in the warm melted wax. So much about quilt making involves the senses of touch and feeling. Even when painting on the crane in my *Georgia* quilt, the interplay of cloth and paint was very different from what that same process would be on hard, stretched canvas. And of course it requires a lot of patience. The greatest gift I have received from the experience of making quilts is patience. There is no hurrying. You may stay up all night to get something done *sooner*, but you can never quilt *faster*.

24 March 1992

I am writing to the librarian in my old hometown of Houston, Mississippi, telling her I cannot manage to display my quilts April 5–11, 1992. Not having heard from her when I wrote a good while ago, and not really feeling too well much of the time since then, I have not gotten as much work done as I hoped. Three of the quilts I planned to display are still here unfinished, and I have given away four of my earlier quilts, which would be hard to gather up quickly. Maybe later.

26 March 1992

I believe Eddie and I have truly enjoyed much of our life together. The enormous problems that cast their shadows on our lives have also made us appreciate the enjoyable moments. And memory also enhances the good times by sort of *airbrushing* the bad.

Today I put four slips of paper in a book with names on them—rubbed from the memorial wall—of men who were with Eddie in Vietnam and died. At the beginning of the book, where I put these slips of paper, are these lines from T.S. Eliot's *Four Quartets:*

> *We die with the dying:*
> *See, they depart, and we go with them.*
> *We are born with the dead:*
> *See, they return, and bring us with them.*

27 March 1992

I feel so positive today, I had to stop and write. I ran into a snag, as I often do with the mathematical side of my projects, in setting the small diamonds around my hexagon quilt, and every one of them had to be *unbasted* and let out a tiny fraction so they could meet end on end in the border. I fudged a little in making them fit around evenly by setting the two center diamonds apart. At first I thought all of my work up to this point had been for nothing. But, as my sister Anne and I once told each other about our sewing, "If you keep at it, there is always *some* way to do what you want to do." (Not necessarily an easy way, but a way.) So while I was taking all of these little diamonds apart and resewing them, I got out the tapes my friend Mildred made for me recently.

These songs, all her favorites, carried me back in time to the days when I listened to the slow, dreamy music of "Georgia on My Mind," "Unforgettable," and "Hawaiian Wedding Song." "Stairway to the Stars" was our senior high school banquet and dance theme. The Johnny Mathis music reminds me of how my friend Ann and I listened to him every time I visited her. Nat King Cole was my favorite when everyone else liked Elvis. "The Impossible Dream," "Crazy," "Melody of Love." Every song was wonderful. It was an unexpectedly emotional experience, which was made more intense by the fact that, as I listened, I was aware that another woman had very carefully picked out these songs and put them together for me, much as I do when sorting and piecing quilts.

At the end of the first tape, Mildred is humming, softly, some strains from the final piece. I can picture her listening to this music—as if we are listening to it together—and know that even though there is a generation between us (for she is my mother's age), we probably are very much alike. As I see myself at twenty in Julie, I see myself at seventy in Mildred. I appliquéd some figures of cats on a shirt for her, and now she has made these tapes for me. And so, as women have done for centuries, we have shared and exchanged little pieces of our lives and bridged the years that divide us.

Most days it is so easy for me to forget the richness of life that I felt it was appropriate here to acknowledge what I feel on a day when my joy and hope are not blocked out by my sickness.

Very nice things are still happening.

28 March 1992

> *Each day, and the living of it, has to be a conscious creation*
> *in which discipline and order are relieved with some play and*
> *pure foolishness.* —May Sarton

I remember reading May Sarton's writing in college. I love the above observation.

Sometimes when I am alone here with FuFu, my fat little dog—alone, that is, except for the other pets—and he jumps up beside me on the couch and puts his head on my knee, I feel such a swell of emotion and comfort. Pee is old and sick now, but FuFu is like my baby. I used to feel sorry for people I saw gushing over a dog—they looked so pathetic—so I am still careful not to gush if anyone is around.

I suspect that when I hold and pet this weird little dog, I am letting go of all my pent-up emotion. I am almost afraid to try to hug *people* anymore with this tube in my face and the bad breath I am

FuFu, late 1980s

certain to have. I hold back from people now, and maybe people hold back from me too; I cannot be sure about this. Eddie still kisses me unexpectedly sometimes, as he always has, but I don't see many people anymore, and I have a sense that most people are a little afraid of me.

Whatever the reason, I hope someone will love FuFu as much as I do when I am gone. He loves being held and talked to. Sometimes when he is just wandering around, he will come over and lean against my leg for me to pat and hug him. This is pure *foolishness* on my part—as May Sarton would say—I am sure.

31 March 1992

> *When you have to make a choice and don't make it, that is in itself a choice.*   —William James

I am going to see my doctor tomorrow. I am feeling better daily and I plan to ask him about some new drugs I have heard about. I told Eddie I hated to seem as if I am grasping for some kind of miracle, since rejecting the idea of having a transplant—I never seriously considered it—but anything that might make life easier would be welcome.

I also want my doctor to sign an absentee ballot request form for me. I want to be sure to vote in the primary, though I feel disappointed in the choices. Politicians in general seem such unsavory people these days, as the character police keep reminding us. Some hoping to be reelected to Congress have been writing bad checks at the public's expense. Others' private lives are exposed as being no better than sleazy soap operas, and still other candidates have earned the nicknames of "loony" and "moonbeam." All those *suits* and so much nonsense and wasted money.

7 April 1992

> *And remember, we all stumble, every one of us. That's why*
> *it's a comfort to go hand in hand.*   —E.K. Brough

Tonight one of my nieces called up very upset about financial matters. She is in a real bind. How do an aunt and uncle know what is the right thing to do? My heart says to help her without any question; my head says try to teach her something about responsibility. Eddie and I talked it over for a long time and went with our hearts.

7 May 1992

Tonight when I saw a commercial on TV, I suddenly felt this flood of loss and pain. The ad was for *paint*, of all things! It was so unexpected, and I felt so overwhelmed. *Paint.* I can't believe this is what triggered it. But Eddie and I always painted the house together. It was crazy, I suppose, but somehow it always felt so good after the hard, physical labor. Like working in the yard, or wallpapering rooms, it was very satisfying on a level that I never really understood. Maybe it was some kind of nest-building, primal thing. Whatever it was,

Patsy with her parents, Peabody Hotel, Memphis, 1947

tonight I was struck by how long it has been since I could do anything like this at all, and how much I miss it—even the arguing with Eddie about what to do and how to do it—and the aching back and muscles. All of it. Once, when it was hot, I would come inside every once in a while and lie stretched out flat on the living room floor, soaking wet.

I have had to replace, to try to replace, the physical pleasures with other things that are not physical. But can you do this? Can you ever replace sight with touch? Signing for hearing? Wheels for legs? Memory for active experience?

None of the other neighborhood women ever helped paint their homes as far as I know. No doubt they would not understand my sense of loss, or why my memories of those hot, humid days up on a ladder are such good ones for me.

17 May 1992

Today my family celebrated my birthday. There seems to be a lot of tension among us now, and still they came over, and as I watched them, I wished there was something I could do or say to let them know how I love them. My sisters and their families are probably why I have had these forty-nine years. They have accepted me just as I am. So have my brother and his wife, who are almost a generation and many miles away. They all took the time and trouble to come to my quilt show last year, and I am sure they could not know how much this meant to me.

This week Mother was tearfully telling me (which is not uncommon) about myself as a child. She said the doctors told her I had a diagnosis of *bronchiectasis* and the outlook wasn't good at all because it was usually only seen in old people with damaged lungs. Today they say it is *cystic fibrosis*. There was, and is, a need to give a name to the inexplicable. Yet whatever they call it, I know how socially unacceptable sickness is. This is probably part of why I spent most of these forty-nine years trying to pretend my illness didn't exist. Only now it is impossible to pretend anymore, attached as I am to oxygen all the time and as old as this "child" is feeling.

Sometimes I feel I have lived too long. I used to have so much nervous energy. When I was tired, I could still keep going and get things done. Now I need to sit down just to talk. I used to like being involved in life. Now, the family brings life to me: a quilt book, a poem, a book of short stories—and best of all, gold sandals that say, "I still know who you are."

21 May 1992

Today I realized I *have* been better since last September, when I saw this woman who says she's a healer. I was hospitalized in October 1991 and February 1992—but since then, not once. In the twelve months prior to seeing her, I was hospitalized eight or nine times.

24 May 1992

I didn't go to my niece Angie's birthday party at Mother's today. I just could not get it together. Sometimes I feel so useless when I

Pat's paternal grandparents Eugene and Nellie Gillespie Roberts and her father Richard, in front of their Nashville home, around 1920

need help dressing and bathing that, rather than ask for help and show my weakness, I just attempt less and do the best I can.

I feel bad about missing the party, though. Last week Angie came for my birthday and brought me a book of short stories, which I love. Eddie did go over and take a gift. He says he doesn't enjoy things without me. I wonder if this is possible, when I am such a mess now, but I do appreciate his saying it anyway.

He and I used to square off, and I would say I would leave, as I had before when marriage hadn't worked out. But now I know that what these earlier marriages lacked were time and determination.

This marriage has had both time and determination. I never really wanted to leave it. Now, of course, I cannot.

26 May 1992

I began the antibiotics again here at home, so it meant stomach cramps, indigestion, and anxiety until I can adjust. FuFu's sick, too. Maybe sympathy sickness? I can't breathe; he snorts and rattles. God help us. Are we somehow locked in this together? This afternoon he seemed to be choking across the room, and as I went toward him I tripped and fell and lost my oxygen. I squeezed him until he could breathe again, then suddenly I couldn't get my own breath. Dr. Death, where are you?

I wish I had a dollar for every time I have thought *"I can't make it any longer"*—and yet I do. Why is it I keep on going? What more can I learn from this disease? I can't write anymore now. I feel too upset. I can't even work on my quilts half the time now. Later.

4 June 1992

I asked Mother the other day if she would help me baste together the layers of batting, backing, and quilt tops that my great-grandmother gave her when she first married, and she has just recently given to me. I'm not sure I can even do it alone now because it is difficult for me to lean and bend over.

Mother spent the day here and it was nice. We don't seem to step on each other's toes so much anymore. I showed her the two quilt tops, which I had cleaned up and repaired and finished off with borders. I am trying to find someone to quilt them for me—and for her.

This is the day my father was born in 1915. He died fifty-one years later, and for all of my twenty-three years with him, he was a complete enigma. For as long as I can remember, I knew (or believed) that my father had wanted to be a painter. My grandmother kept some of the paintings he did hanging in her living room long after he had quit wanting to be an artist and had become a doctor. I never quite figured out why he had changed his plans. I understood that one or both of his parents wanted him to study medicine, but whether he also had ceased to love art was unclear and today seems unlikely, and maybe that's what went wrong in his life. Maybe he just followed someone else's dream instead of his own. The only interest he ever really showed in me was when I became interested in painting and art in high school. I could always lose myself in drawing, or painting, or designing something. Hours would pass before I knew it, and I found this to be true years later when I went back to college. It's just as true today. There is something that draws me into this work and keeps me going.

Mother reminded me this was my father's birthday, but I also thought about him today because I received a letter from my niece Meg in which she mentions genetic inheritance. When writing her earlier, I had said that because she has my middle name, I feel as if a part of me will go on with her into the next century. Her letter was touching, and it made me think about how much we are shaped by family and people with whom we grow up.

8 June 1992

Today I received a card from Sarah saying she had gotten the silk-screen print I had framed for her as a gift. I had forgotten about my print, which I have intended to use as a model for something similar in cloth and thread. It has a human shape in motion behind a grid of bars, a trapped figure reaching out and moving beyond. I called it *Private Dancer* (and thought of Meg). In the print, the several androgynous figures merge to juxtapose the linear stasis with the organic movement. In cloth, I planned to make a diptych or triptych by stretching fabric over a frame in two or three pieces. It is still in my head, but it seemed at the time to stray too far beyond the traditional boundaries of quilt making. I am leaving the idea behind me for now.

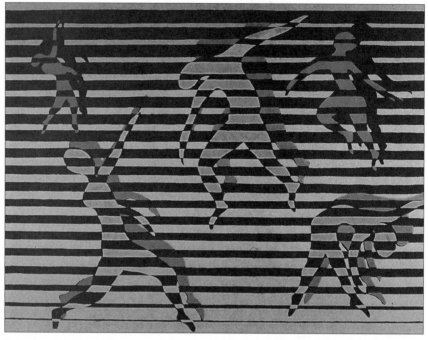

Private Dancer, *silk-screen on paper, 14" x 19", idea for* Symphony *series*

17 June 1992

I realize that sticking clippings and cards in random places in this journal means that there is always the danger of dropping the book and scattering everything, which is why it still seems like a good idea, like not keeping the dates in order. My life and my thoughts are *never* orderly, so why should my journal be?

This week a friend died, and I am having a hard time believing it. When I can, I will write about her in my larger journal. I was supposed to leave *her*. *She* was not supposed to leave me.

I cannot think about this now.

An unexpected problem has reared its head, causing quilting groups around the U.S. much concern. Quilts are now being made in China and sold here for nothing compared to what our quilters charge. The Smithsonian seems to have started it by sending some of its patterns abroad to be duplicated by prisoners or women who make twenty-five cents an hour, before the goods are shipped back here for sale as Americana. Soon American stores were doing the same thing and making big profits. Now if Mary Smith should ever decide to sew her name on one of these quilts (though of course, she would *never*), how will families who have quilts left to them ever know which are authentic and which are imports? If our history is unclear, think of future generations trying to separate quilts made by Great-aunt Agnes from those made in Communist China? The labors of love from work by "slave labor"? The relics of pleasant hours spent in quiet contemplation from the record of desperate hours of exploitation? It will be a terrible job for the future.

24 June 1992

I will have three of my quilts at the quilt show at Franklin Park Friday and Saturday. I will try to go with Mother and Katie to see it. They told me there will be approximately 150 quilts shown. I want to see them so badly.

25 June 1992

I don't know if this journal is the place for a death notice, but what is the proper place for the unexpected death (from an aneurysm) of a forty-four-year-old woman who has been my friend for more than twenty years? I was supposed to die first, so I know a little part of how her parents feel. She came to all my quilt shows, and one of the last times I saw her was when she dropped by the house and brought me some fabric scraps. So the loss does belong in this quilting journal. If quilting is about connections, then it must also be about the separations and losses of continuity that occur when we least expect it. Edvard Munch said that illness, madness, and death were the "black angels" that kept watch over him. He tried to transform them into visual metaphors for the human condition. I think of Munch because so much pain was expressed in his work, and I am feeling so much pain now. And, like him, I want to do something, to create something, to express this.

I am copying the letter I wrote her family in here to remind myself of the first days I realized she was gone forever. Later I plan to make something to remember her by—something perhaps like the AIDS quilt—that says, "*You meant a lot to us and you left us far too soon.*"

> Dear Mr. and Mrs. __,
>
> I have thought all afternoon about what to say to you. I want to tell you how much Eddie and I both loved Linda. I feel I have to say this to you because I regret never having said this to Linda. Because she has always been there whenever I needed her—a shoulder to cry on or someone to laugh with—I assumed Linda would always be there. I hope, and want to believe, that she knew we loved her.
>
> We go back such a long way. Linda was in her twenties when we met. A couple of years later she came to our wedding. In the seventies, while so many of us were recovering from the sixties, Linda always seemed to be the stable, levelheaded one. We shared so many good times. We have a stack of photo albums with pictures of Linda and we would be glad to share them with you if you ever want to see them. Truthfully, these photos and memories have sustained Eddie and me during recent months.
>
> Until the past couple of years Linda and I laughed often about the "way we were"—how naive and idealistic. Some things were only funny in retrospect, and Linda handled the bad breaks in her life better than anyone I know. When I think of her I hear her laughter. In conversations sometimes we would stumble across some awful truth we were glossing over; Linda would hesitate and our eyes would meet and she would burst into laughter. This is the woman I will always remember.

Over the years Linda and I talked about pets we have loved, jobs we sometimes hated, men who confounded us, books we read, our "dolls," her dancing, and my quilting. We talked about our parents and siblings, and if I am absolutely certain of anything about Linda, it is how much she loved and respected you. In times like these, when blaming families for any and everything is a popular pastime, I can honestly say that I never heard Linda say one bad word about her family. Through the years, whenever we talked, she spoke of you often and lovingly.

So many things we shared in years past have run through my mind these last two days. Linda will live on in our memory and we feel fortunate to have known her. I am sure anyone who knew her well feels the same way.

If we can help you in any way now, or in the future, do not hesitate to call us.

Love,

Pat

The unspoken issues, at least in my letter, that Linda and I shared also were childlessness, perceived as an un-American stance in a nation preoccupied with babies and children; the painful experience of divorce (involving poverty and the struggle to get an education); and our female need to experience our sexuality in the absence of marriage, or within it.

19 July 1992

I now have become aware that I cannot keep my personal life and working or artistic life separate in separate journals. Before I realized it, they had begun to overlap. Events such as Linda's death and my hospital stays had gotten mixed up with my quilt notes. So from here on out, I will simply not worry about it.

I am feeling a little better today and this morning I felt so well, I went into the room where I keep all my fabrics and thought about some future ideas for projects. I now have collected many blues for *Memphis Blues*, which I plan to do next. I put my silk and lamé packages with the hand-dyed material for my stained-glass piece. I want it to be reminiscent somehow of O'Keeffe's and Judy Chicago's female imagery, but also have it suggest more traditional work, like the Tiffany, Edwardian, or Victorian stained-glass patterns. I also want to do something in a very traditional pattern like Pioneer Braid or Crazy Patch Squares or strip piecing, but using my most unusual fabrics—the African, hand-dyed, lamé, and Oriental cloth. I want also to use my sun-printed blocks of my grandmother's crochet in some way. There is so much I want to do, and quilt making must be slow and deliberate work because it is the nature of the needle arts. Now to sit down and finish the three quilts I have under way at present. When I begin, sometimes I work all day and feel, as one quilter has written, that I am returning to "mythic patterns and ancient rituals."

Recently a woman from my quilter's guild asked me what I was working on, and I got excited telling her about my newer quilts. She said she was surprised that I still felt like quilting, and I knew I could not explain that I quilt *because* of how I feel, that it provides me with purpose in the midst of the chaos and uncertainty of my life.

I have begun to keep correspondence in here, as I did in my other journal. It is very awkward, and yet it is an important aspect of my existence now. It is my primary connection to people I would otherwise lose touch with. When I am down and I read these letters, they help to bring me back up.

This morning Linda's father called. Eddie and I were still asleep, though it was late. The work on the house has been a strain. Eddie answered and talked to him, and then he spoke to her mother for a while. I pretended to be asleep. As I drifted back, I wondered what we might have done differently if I had known I would end up so confined, and if Linda had known her life would end at forty-four. I think probably we would have done exactly what we did (and what I am still doing): whatever we had to do to survive in a world not always so kind to divorced women, or disabled women, or women with no children to validate their existence as far as most—or many—other women are concerned. And, having said this, I believe we cherished the joy we had, with our extended families, with the men who loved us, and with other special people who came into our lives along the way.

25 July 1992

As the summer of '92 slips away, the presidential campaign heats up. I secured an absentee ballot, but I don't feel hopeful about the whole thing. The country's problems seem to be unsolvable. Can this be true?

Last night I put the finishing touches on Richard and Carol's quilt, *Georgia on My Mind*. This quilt has a southern touch, but is also a nod to O'Keeffe, one of the few women painters of the past to have gained recognition.

It is almost as if I know that I am still alive only because I read what I wrote yesterday or last week, or I see the progress on my quilts, the tiny little stitches I have so perfected now. Sometimes people who examine them closely think they must be done by a machine. They are not. These very small and deliberate stitches are the part of my life over which I still have control.

I remember reading once, "It is not what you are that holds you back, but what you think you are." Maybe in my case I could adjust this to read, "*It is not what you are doing that propels you forward, but what you think you are doing.*"

3 August 1992

Late this afternoon my mother called as I was quilting. She has closed on her home of almost forty years in Mississippi. My husband took her back there to get this settled. I am sure she is both relieved and sad, but what she talks to me about is so unexpected. She has a pile of things brought back from the house that she thinks she will give me. I had asked her for an old photo of her mother and aunt as children in Victorian dress, and this she mentions. But suddenly she is reading to me from my father's various medical certificates—things, she says, she never even knew he studied. She has his "dog tags" and other small items: a pair of kid gloves that belonged to him as a child—a special, gifted, only child. I realized this was some kind of ending or closure for her. For myself, I hope it will let me make some kind of peace with a father I never understood—perhaps because I never wanted to, fearing I might see myself if I looked too closely. Over and over I think to myself, "*Death ends a life, but not a relationship.*"

Then I found myself telling my mother about having seen some terrible scenes on the news showing Africa's boat people, hundreds of starving Somalians trying to leave their war-torn country. Their homeland has nothing left: no schools, no center of government, no way to feed them. The images were so disturbing and unexpected, they caught me completely off guard and had been on my mind all day. I told my mother that it made me realize how fortunate I really am. I have the best medical care available, air-conditioning, extra oxygen, people and dogs I love around me. I needed to remind myself, when I am down as much as I have been lately, what a struggle some humans have from birth to death. I just needed to be jolted into examining my own situation and appreciating what I do have. Then Mother told me the strangest thing; my father had said something similar when he was very sick and near death and saw the terrible images of the Vietnam war on the TV news. She prefaced this story by saying, as she has said before, "You remind me of your father."

My mother also tells me (through my husband) that she remembered how I ran away when I was growing up. (I wonder how their six-hour trip has cut through walls of silence.) She told him that I first ran away when I was seven or eight, taking my sister Anne with me, pulling her in a wagon; and the last time, when I was fifteen, taking this same sister in the family car. I *always* ran, or tried to run, to my grandmother. It's hard to remember why I ran. When I was small, I was running from my parents; as an adult, from myself. Maybe it was all about the same thing.

There is an Oriental proverb: "If fate throws a knife at you, there are two ways of catching it—by the blade and by the handle." I think my hands were very scarred by the time I figured this out. I nearly bled to death.

9 August 1992

I have recently perfected the quilting stitch, at long last. It has been very difficult for me. I had been using improvised methods, which were slow and sometimes uneven. But after I gave my niece Julie my little book, *How to Quilt*, she picked it right up and showed me how. This technique is important because it is quicker and keeps the stitches more even. I have always been more enthusiastic about the designing end of quilt making but secretly felt disappointed in myself for not being able to do the stitching as well as I felt I should. Now I am getting 10-12 stitches per inch, which is pretty good, and my quilts for Julie and Richard and Carol will, in every respect, be my best so far.

24 August 1992

The month is going fast. I have not done as much quilting as I had hoped. I have been so caught up instead with straightening out my sewing room that today I am even going through boxes of old photographs and putting them into albums. This has gotten me into reliving the past, of course, as I look at the pictures of high school days and friends, an early marriage that did not last, my snapshots of the younger siblings growing up, and old, brown photos from the early 1900s of grandparents and a great-grandmother. I am putting some of these photographs here in this journal.

I needed to make this escape from the present this week because it has been very painful. Our old dog Pee Dee died. He and I had been living within an ever-decreasing perimeter. Every so often he would stand up and look around, as if he had forgotten where he was, then sit down again and eventually lie down and fall asleep. The last days, I had to hand-feed him and give him water from a

Pee Dee

dropper, and he cried and whimpered all night. I was answering the Crisis line, and sometimes he cried if I got caught up in a phone call and stopped patting him. I felt his suffering at the end was my fault, and I wish I had had the courage to let him be put to sleep. But I loved him so much it seemed like a betrayal. After he died, August 20, I felt that a part of me was gone. I sat with him on the floor, his familiar territory, all night and into the early morning when he died. The worst part of life is loss and letting go. Eddie said, later, our dog was like me because "he loved life." I was amazed when he said this, since I am not always so sure anymore that I love life. But the truth is, I *do*. When it comes right down to it, I *do*. And now I will miss my old dog, who loved to run and bark, who was my smartest dog, who always wanted to be close to me, and whom I loved as much as if he were human. He was truly caught here with me "in the net of life and time, fellow prisoner of the splendor and travail of the earth," as someone recently wrote in the Humane Society newsletter. I still can't believe he is gone.

18 September 1992

I wrote to Cynthia for the first time in a year (almost), and she wrote back. It was so good to know she is out there. I have so completely lost touch with people who lifted my spirits and shared my celebration when I had my show and encouraged me to keep going when I thought I could not. I heard from Audrey this spring telling me how they hung my quilt and also the letter, now framed, that I wrote them about it. I *need* to keep in touch, and it is so difficult now.

21 September 1992

I have had Pee Dee on my mind. It has been one month since he died.

When I began writing just now, I looked up and FuFu was sitting there, staring at me. He always looks sad, but actually he is always happy, enthusiastic. I got him seven years ago after our shih tzu, Lottie, died. Pee Dee was her puppy, and he was ailing. (The vet said heart

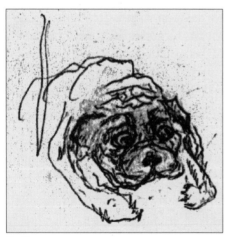

FuFu

problems.) But Pee Dee perked up when FuFu came roaring in—FuFu, whom we could hold in one hand. Later, of course, we acquired Smokey, a small poodle, to keep him from being put to sleep. He is now fifteen years old, so he will probably join Pee Dee in the not-too-distant future, although he seems well. He sleeps all day.

23 September 1992

A woman called me and wanted me to make a whole cloth quilt for her, but I told her I only sew for my family or people I am close to. I cannot imagine the slow, painstaking work of designing and putting together and finishing being done for money alone. What price could I possibly put on my tiny stitches, my sense of design, when the arduous undertaking of making a quilt by myself from start to finish requires that it be nothing less than a work of love?

Early October 1992

I felt I should write here about these old photos I have included. My great-grandmother, grandmother, and father are here. My father was an artist who became a doctor. When he was very ill and could not practice medicine anymore, he drew ink sketches for Anne and me. I can still see his trembling hand in the lines. I can see his attempt to reach us in the end, and I am glad I can see this now.

I knew none of these relatives, with the exception of my father, grandmother, great-grandmother, and one great-uncle, standing behind my grandmother. The photos speak to me of harsh times I never experienced. My great-grandmother was married to a Civil War veteran. She had so many children I have lost count. She married, I believe, three times, survived all of her husbands and several children, and lived her final days in my grandmother's home, where she continued to quilt. Quilting was most likely the one constant thread running through her long, long life. I have a photograph of my grandmother and her sister, Mary, as infants, propped up on a crazy quilt.

But I was close not to this grandmother, but to my mother's

mother. And with all the security and unconditional love my maternal grandmother gave me, it was easy not to care about these *country people* on my father's side. I only began to wonder more about them, particularly my great-grandmother, when I started to quilt. As I am writing this, I know I am trying to find my roots and trace my inheritance.

My youngest nephew sent me a card while I was in the hospital once. On the envelope he wrote "PATS WHY?"—a child's play on words that could not have been more appropriate for an aunt who spent so much time asking *why?* Not so much why she had this lung disease, but why she continued to live despite it. I have asked myself where this resilience and hidden strength came from, and how it has overcome the self-destructive aspect of my nature. Has it come from my grandmother and her mother, who both lived well into their nineties? Of course it is always impossible to know why, but equally impossible not to ask the question when life becomes very difficult.

4 November 1992

I see I have skipped most of October and wonder why. Perhaps it is because I have been writing my nieces so much, and I can only justify so much time spent with pen and paper. Or maybe I just haven't that much to say. I feel, on a personal level, that I am slowing down very gradually, but, strangely, at the same time I have felt that I have more creative energy. I finished the final design of my Web and Weaving block for *Victorian Echo*. There is still a lot left to be done on it, but already I have an idea for another project, a series based on harmony and movement in color. I have begun to use colored pencils and to lay out the arrangement of color on tissue over a grid of squares. Somehow I seem to be coming up with all of these possibilities, and I am actually finishing Julie's quilt, too.

One of the little girls next door sent me a rock, by Eddie, that she said was "very pretty." I put it in my sewing box. I cannot throw children's drawings away, either. I have a desk full of them.

*Great-grandmother
Dora Gillespie and
grandchildren in
the 1930s*

December 1992

Some months back, I quit writing regularly in my yellow quilt
journal. I am not sure why, but it seems to have to do with feeling
stuck and unable to grow or plan. More and more, I have felt a need
to feel better, not only physically and emotionally, but especially
spiritually. When each of my sisters gave me a *Plain and Simple* journal, I realized that now is the time for me to focus on this concern.

These *Plain and Simple* journals will by their very nature allow
me to speak of my search for meaning and to find my way as I progress
on my journey. Since I am no longer able to talk to people very well,
I will talk things out here in hopes of finding some spiritual guid-
ance to help me endure this final stage of my illness with grace.

Earlier, I worried about my family and others seeing me sick and distracted for a long time. I was afraid they would forget the *me* who once enjoyed life, with all of its celebrating and loving. Now I don't worry about it as much because it is sometimes hard for *me* to remember the person I was.

Now I need to understand what matters and what does not. I want to avoid the distractions, but enjoy the important time spent with others. I also want to be quiet enough to feel the Amazing Grace in my life. I want to believe that all the pain and difficulty in my life have had some meaning that eludes me now but will become clear before I leave if I *listen* closely enough.

I had a brief romance with the Amish while taking an anthropology course in college. As I read about them, and wrote a couple of papers, I was briefly transported back to a time in my childhood when I was very religious. At that time, I wanted to be *so good* that I would go straight to heaven if I died on the spot, and apparently having some doubts, even then, about my strength to fend off temptation, I decided to become a nun as the surest path to perfect holiness. Often I have wondered how I became so cynical and gave up my early belief in a just and loving God. Was it because I strayed so far from the light myself and allowed the dark side of my nature to obliterate whatever light there was? I suppose I felt that if I could never be good enough, there was no point in trying to be good at all.

But maybe it doesn't matter now why, or how, or even if. Maybe now I just need to stop and listen, and if I listen hard enough, and keep my heart open, and give others the respect I want for myself, in time I will feel a presence that gives my experience meaning.

I keep working on the quilts. Julie's is almost finished.

29 December 1992

I have got to start writing again. I tried this year to have family for dinner on both Thanksgiving and Christmas. It is such a lot of hard work. Mother and my younger sisters helped with Thanksgiving, but everyone was worn out by Christmas. Still, all in all, it was worth the effort. Everyone seemed to enjoy the time together. I wanted to try to do this again. I thought last year I never wood (would). I am managing better now.

I have started to make strange mistakes like the one I just made in writing and speaking. Maybe I am just paranoid. I try to be careful, when writing letters especially.

I believe my failure to live up to my own expectations, as far as my life with God went, occurred around the age of thirteen. Now, looking back, I can see and understand the emotional upheavals in my life during puberty.

My youngest sister was injured while riding behind me on my bicycle. I swerved and her foot went into the spokes, and part of her toe was cut off. At the time when she screamed and I saw the blood, I thought I had cut half her foot off. She was three, so her foot was very small. I ran home with her, and they took her to the hospital. I remember sitting on the stairs in the hours that followed praying she would not be crippled. And I struck a bargain with God. If she were allowed to walk, I would definitely become a nun. An idea turned into a promise. If this, then that. From that point on, my life was full of broken promises. I never considered why a God, to whom I had lied so many times, would keep on granting my wishes, or why I felt He was turning His back on me when my promises got no response. But eventually I stopped bargaining as my sense of God's presence faded.

But now I need something more, some source of strength I can trust to help me cope. I am often afraid that after spending so much of my life in running away from a faith and failing to live up to my potential for good, it is not possible for me to have God in my life. Yet I want so much to believe that God can still be there for me.

Several months ago I began reading at night from a very old prayer book. I have trouble with the language, but it is the way I remember my earlier God. So much has changed in the Catholic church since then, but this was the only way I knew God. I feel this is a beginning for me. I must somehow go back to *my* beginning and hope I have enough time. I am taking time twice a day to think about finding a spiritual connection that can help me.

The distractions in my life have been removed one by one. After all the early attempts at marriage, the jobs I had, the friends I made, the years in college, the trips, I am now almost fifty and connected by a fifty-foot tube to a tank of oxygen that prevents me from walking around with my dogs or with my husband. I *can* write and work on my quilts, which have helped me understand how ephemeral life really is. What I must do now is use this time to recover what I lost so long ago. It is not God I must recover but faith and trust that whatever happens, I will be able to endure it.

Sometimes I am so afraid that as I get worse I will make life more difficult for my husband. My prayer today is that I won't make life more difficult for him by my own anxiety and that he will *see* me find peace.

4 January 1993

Last night, very late, we were talking and Eddie started remembering things we have done together. It worries me somehow, but still I have to admit I love to hear him do this. Eddie never mentions bad times or blames me for any unhappiness in our lives. I have come to understand that this is how he is surviving what we are going through. In a spiritual sense he is teaching me that if I will be quiet, and less angry, I can appreciate the time we have had and especially the laughter that we shared.

8 January 1993

Tonight, for some reason, I remembered a time in my roaring twenties when I ended up with a cab leaving me at my grandmother's in the middle of the night. Had I had a wreck and been to an emergency room? I don't even really remember what happened, my life was in such turmoil then. But I *do* remember my grandmother that night. The only thing she asked me was, "Are you all right?" When I said, "Yes," she simply led me back to her bed. I was sick, and far from all right. I was so lost I felt beyond redemption. Yet as I began to fall asleep, I felt my grandmother lying beside me put her arms around me. I went to sleep with her patting me the way she had in earlier years.

This was the kind of a God I wanted, a God who would enfold me—not physically, but spiritually. A presence, like my grandmother, in whom I could always find comfort. I am sure it is my own fault I never felt this. Maybe I wanted, expected, too much. But I know I am still looking for this comfort, this feeling that I am supremely loved.

Eddie has replaced my grandmother in this stage of my lung disease. When I am very sick, he is always nurturing. I can't stand myself during the endless coughing spells and all that goes with them. He is so patient, I cannot imagine how I could have survived these last two years without him. It may be that my grandmother and Eddie have been gifts from God, and if I can see this, I will understand that God does comfort me. It is hard to believe I am all alone in this struggle. No, I would have been dead long ago, I am sure.

This year, I have concocted a sort of regimen that has eased some of my physical problems, though if I have company or an unusually long phone call, I still have trouble regaining my sense of security and a breathing pattern I can manage. For a long time, when I had a bad coughing spell, I had trouble getting my breath back. I would feel desperate and panicky until, gradually, I began to take steps to get through these episodes. I would count, breathing out as long and hard as I could, then breathe in. I began to use the six-hour spray on a regular basis, not just when I panicked. I also—and this is a key part of my new routine—began drinking a lot of water, glasses and glasses. Strangely this water eliminated my chronic side pain. My joint pain and even the chronic indigestion have also gotten better.

It is hard to believe that water has done this—has brought me so much relief—but as far as I can see, it has. Did I stumble on this miracle by sheer accident, or was it another gift from God? Am I so skeptical that I want to be blind to God's help in my life? Does a voice in me still say, "I wouldn't need help in my life if it weren't so terrible?"

11 January 1993

What an awful day! I blew my program of trying to maintain a sense of peace for the sake of my spirituality, if you will.

Beverly was cleaning, the dog was barking, Eddie was trying to install a phone where I didn't want it and wouldn't listen to me at all. I went crazy. I snatched the phone and I said, "I don't want an extra phone in case of emergency, I don't want to be stuck here with the damn phone, I don't want … " It was really ugly.

Eddie was mad for a while; then my asthma kicked in, of course, so that subdued me rather quickly. It helped having a witness to my temper fit, but I still feel bad about the overreaction. I think it was partly a buildup of other things. I hear people say all the time that they pray over something, or turn it over to God. Why doesn't this work for me? Okay, I prayed. Okay, I turned it over. Why don't I feel a bit different?

I guess I will do what I used to do when I was a child. Start fresh tomorrow.

12 January 1993

Tonight I saw a young woman on TV playing the piano, and she made me think about an old high school friend. We got in so much trouble together, running away—not *to* anything, but *from* everything to find ourselves. We were *bad* girls, we thought.

But she could play the piano so beautifully, could just sit down and play. She had such a gift, and she worked as hard as she played.

Both of us did. I painted, drew pictures, and loved everything that had to do with art. I really believed in my own ability when I was young. We both thought we were destined to *be something*. And both of us, somehow, soon shifted our passions. All that energy, that creative energy, was wasted (a harsh word, but what else can I say?) on men: short men, tall men, smart men, dumb men—just men. Both of us married too quickly, and in the end, our lives were empty. She has three beautiful grown children, but she is unmarried now. And when I last saw her and asked if she still plays the piano, she said, "Only when I'm at Mother's, and she asks me to quit after a while because it makes her nervous."

I have no children, of course, but feel so lucky that I finally got to go to college to study art and have found out what love is about. All because I have a serious, long-term illness. Would I have ever looked at my life if I had not had to deal with this lung disease? First, it took away my ability to work outside my home, then certainly my ability to function even here as a normal person. But it gave me time to think about what is important and what is not.

19 January 1993

A friend of Eddie's called him tonight, and I talked to him a minute. I had been meaning to call him, but didn't quite know how to approach him. I had called him when I was in the hospital quite a while back and had asked him, in so many words, to "keep an eye on Eddie" because I felt then, March 1991, that I was very close to the edge, physically and mentally. I truly believed I would not last much longer, and here I have had more than a year without hospitalization. Now I wanted to let him off the hook and told him I almost felt embarrassed, but was very grateful for the turnaround. He said not to worry about it. He has been through some bad times himself, and he understands. He is such a nice guy and was very kind about my situation.

21 January 1993

Bills due, time to get the tax stuff together, and I have been distracted by my new *Symphony* project. I keep working on it, but still need some unifying device to bring the four pieces together, and I cannot come up with *the* answer. I even dreamed about it last night.

I feel exceptionally well. I think the cold weather helps. I notice when I am doing better, I don't think quite so much about a spiritual life. I am busy, so I suppose I don't think as deeply or am not so given over to introspection. I still want my life to have meaning, and I do not want to waste time on anger, or fear, or doing *anything* that will hurt someone else.

1 February 1993

I am so grateful for these good weeks, or is it months? I don't remember when I began to feel better, but my easier breathing has softened the hard edges of my daily existence almost as imperceptibly as one day leads into the next. People who see me now notice I am different. I even went to Anna's birthday Saturday without too much trouble.

Of course, I *couldn't* think of seeing a dentist! I lost that tooth recently because I sat here in pain, taking Tylenol, until it was too late to save it. Sometimes I am so stupid, but I felt I could not manage the trip and dental procedures. When the bone became infected, I got there. I need to be able to make more sensible decisions. The dentist and woman who cleaned my teeth wore gloves and masks, while I wore my oxygen. Life is complicated.

10 February 1993

Today I saw a clip on TV about Michael Jackson's tribute to Ryan White ... "Gone Too Soon." The teenager died with AIDS. It made me stop and think about my own longevity with an illness that has killed and still kills so many *young* people. It reminded me of the value of every day I have. It reminded me to appreciate the time I have now, the family, my husband, people I have met. If I had died when I was young, I would have missed *so much*: the affection of my nieces, getting to know my mother at an age when we both are calmer, going to college. The list goes on.

15 February 1993

In the years since my husband and I began our relationship, I have grown up and changed as the world has been changed by the course of events. A U.S. president, facing impeachment, resigned. The Soviet Union collapsed, as did the Berlin Wall. And AIDS became our world's deadly enemy (as cystic fibrosis is mine). We came through the "sexual revolution" of the sixties, thinking we had put it behind us, only to find thousands dying of AIDS these twenty years later. There is also unrest as developing nations struggle with chaos in government. Even our country now faces high unemployment, rising numbers of homeless people and families, and an inadequate health care system. In these years, women's rights and needs also came to the fore, but were soon drawing opposition as the backlash set in. Oh—and I almost forgot—a national debt most of us cannot really fathom.

But now, to get on to what I can do something about, in my own small way. I can hardly cure all the world's ills, but I can write about what I know and what I have experienced and discovered as a woman, and try to embody this knowledge in my art for the next generation. The hours that I have put into this work wouldn't be believed. Sometimes I work until 3 a.m. Sometimes I wake up and begin again even before I comb my hair. I often dream about something I am trying to work out. I want my quilts to be held and touched and have made them strong, stronger than any canvas I ever painted.

20 February 1993

I have been feeling so sick today that I do not know how I will get past it. I want to live a real life, to walk through a vegetable market and simply touch things; to feel sand between my toes at the ocean's edge, where we spent so much time summers long ago; to experience an embrace without the awkwardness of plastic tubing that reminds me I have already said "good-bye" and those I would embrace have already let me go.

I am having a rotten day, and all I have is the comfort of my fat, warm, soft dog. Maybe he's my salvation. He doesn't pull back when I hug him. Neither does my husband, but he is too careful now. Oh— I won't write anymore. I can't stand being like this.

22 February 1993

I have been watching this wonderful, if sometimes difficult-to-understand, three-part series, "Healing and the Mind," with Bill Moyers. One of the doctors involved in the research said his devotion to medical research was rooted in his feelings for his mother, who had had polio as a young person and was still sick a lot while he was growing up. He had seen her pull through many bouts of respiratory illness through sheer determination. She would just grit her teeth and stick out her chest and recover. He said he had wanted to understand what had made her survival possible and use this to help other people, but he still does not understand. He thinks it is really impossible to tell what helps a patient survive on an individual basis. I have pretty much come to the same conclusion despite my persistence in asking the question, "Why am I still alive?"

When my brother looked through some albums I put together last summer and for the first time saw relatives he never knew, he said, "Wow, they sure look tough!" I had to agree. I knew that my grandmother and great-grandmother lived well into their nineties, though my grandmother was always considered frail and sickly. As a childhood friend of hers said at her funeral, folks never expected Nell to live so long. She had high blood pressure, migraine headaches, ate nothing but sweets, and did not like people very much, and this included her relatives. Her mother and husband died in

1961; my father, her only son, died a few years later. She lived on for many years after these losses. She lived alone, on her own, until a couple of years before she died. Why and how she ever kept going is a mystery.

26 February 1993

I remember a teacher I had in business school, circa 1962–63. She had had polio and was probably in her thirties or forties. It was difficult to tell in my own early twenties. She wore large braces on her legs and had almost to drag herself along on metal crutches that were buckled onto her arms. One day she came in as usual, making a lot of noise in the classroom, which was suddenly very quiet, and when she went to sit down, she somehow lost her balance and fell. Some people laughed—out of nervousness, I expect—but nobody knew what to do. Since everyone thought she was mean, some probably felt she deserved to fall. I don't remember how this poor woman got up or anything else, but I felt so bad about it, and felt bad for such a long time, that it remains my primary memory of that period in my own life. My sympathy came less from any affection or kindness in my heart than from knowing what physical illness could do to the psyche. I knew what it felt like to be *defective* and embarrassed by your body and its ravages. There are probably people who think *I* am mean, for it is very hard to take time to smile and be considerate of others when you are trying to hold on, to make it through another hour yourself. I know this is one reason I chose to work at the Crisis Center; there I *have* to slow down and soften and listen to others. Long-term sickness and its physical impairments cause you to spend an inordinate amount of time in conversation with yourself about how you are going to get from here to there.

10 March 1993

I need to be in the hospital now, but I am afraid of beginning the cycle—that downward spiral—again. I am comfortable here with

111

*Great-grandmother Dora Gillespie, Grandmother Nellie Gillespie Roberts,
Pat's father Richard, and other members of the Gillespie-Roberts clan*

FuFu and Eddie, and in the hospital the IVs and beeping machines
keep me in a netherworld where sleep is interrupted and the food is
very good. This last point scares me the most because whenever I am
trying to persuade myself to go back, I always think, *"The food is not
bad, and they bring it to you and take the dishes away."* I've come to *this*
pitiful state of affairs! I need to see the hospital as a safe place where
I can get help, but I don't anymore. They are always short staffed,
and more and more, the IV nurses seem unskilled. Spiritually I am
not doing too well, either. I read prayers every night, but I am still
soul sick and confused. The other night on the radio I heard a de-
bate about whether or not God exists. One man said he found it
hard to believe there was a supreme being somewhere who took a
personal interest in each of five billion people. I guess that's my problem. I want somehow to feel that I am heard and understood. This is
a lot to ask when I sometimes find it hard to feel this even about my

doctor and husband. But I am trying to hang in there and have faith that I will be comforted, if I seek comfort. This is all I want now. No more miracles.

23 March 1993

I am almost sure that I need to be in the hospital. The good days have to outnumber the bad days, or I am in trouble. This is how I decide when it's time to check myself in for antibiotics. It's a quality-of-life-based formula I worked out for myself years ago. Only this time, I have been fudging and making excuses.

First, ever so slightly, I started to make it harder for a day to qualify as a bad one. It used to be that a "bad day" was when I could not quit coughing by noon. Then I gave myself until afternoon before I had to be cleared up enough to function. Never mind that whenever it took me that long, I felt very tired the rest of the day. Now, it is very late at night before I am cleared up (if even then), and I cannot remember when physical activity was not an exhausting ordeal.

26 March 1993

My doctor mentioned lung transplants the last time I saw him. I told him I didn't want to consider it, but now in my present misery, I am reading a book by a transplant surgeon. I cannot even imagine what it would be like to breathe normally. My life would change so much. It would make me a new person, if it worked. Would I be like the deaf person who could not stand the noise when his hearing was restored? I don't think so. Would I have to find a whole new focus for my life? It is almost too difficult to ponder. I have, for a long, long time, had this fantasy of running and dancing, as I was able to do until I was about thirty. Even now I "slow dance" (alone) sometimes (on good days), which some might say speaks to my mental deterioration. I guess it is normal to grasp at straws, but as I hear more about transplants, I hope my rational self will control my emotional self.

Of course at one time I could not have imagined walking around with an oxygen tube in my nose. I once said I would never go that far. "I would just throw in the towel." Well, I reconsidered, and that is what is so difficult. When you are at the end of your rope, that small, weak thread that offers some hope is awfully tempting.

19 April 1993

I have had such a difficult week. I had a couple of good days around Easter but have not done well since. I have an appointment with my doctor Wednesday.

Mother called a little while ago. She wants to have her priest visit me. I am so confused about this issue, too. I know she will feel better, my uncle will feel better, and maybe I am finally at a point where I will feel better if I can put an end to the old misgivings, anger, and pain. I need to get past that time in my life when I felt God had let me down, the time when I decided that there was no God. On the other hand, I have always believed in the human spirit and the basic goodness of people because there have *always* been the right people for me when I needed them.

27 April 1993

I am reading *The Puzzle People* by a transplant surgeon, Thomas Starzl, who writes that "every patient who went through the experience of receiving someone else's organ … was a puzzle." Nobody could predict how well the new and old pieces would fit together. "Many died. Some found the world a better and kinder place than they had ever known before. Others encountered a cruel swamp in which their vulnerability was turned against them in ways they could not have imagined."

I am supposed to meet my transplant surgeon tomorrow between 9 and 10 a.m. I am trying to do everything the right way, but I am so afraid. *I need have no misgivings.* How could I *not* have misgivings? I am fifty, and I feel this is too old for such an enormous surgery. *I will leave it up to them. No! I* will decide after listening to what everyone involved in the procedure has to say, including myself.

5 May 1993

I am now again working daily on the "desert quilt" for Richard and Carol. I will call it *Georgia on My Mind,* my nod to Georgia O'Keeffe, who died the year I finished my art studies. I have used her ram's skull motif and desert background. O'Keeffe might smile, I suspect, at my presumption in drawing from her work and experience for the sake of a quilt. Yet she herself said that the challenge she faced was to work within given boundaries to preserve and extend tradition. In my quilt, the harshness and beauty of the desert are expressed in the darkness and color and light of my brilliant sky at sunset or sunrise, overcast with a desert storm. I consider this a fabric painting. I ordered hand-dyed fabrics from a small company in

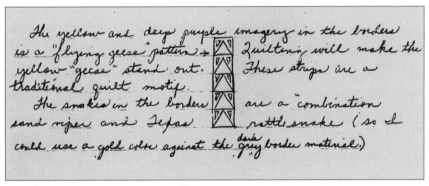

Sketch for Georgia on My Mind

Alaska and pieced them together until the sky was right. Since my own lungs will not allow me to mix my own dyes these days, this company, a man-and-wife operation, helped me out. They have also furnished the color progressions for my *Symphony* series.

I feel I *must* work very hard on getting this information down and completing this quilt as I approach what I see as my final stretch.

Swirling in my mind, or what is left of it, is this latest development: my lung specialist has sent me to a transplant surgeon for consultation. He has already talked to this surgeon about me. What did they say? I don't know that I want to know, really. It is such a long shot. In the beginning, I refused even to consider it, but now I have agreed to some initial testing. Enough about that; it casts a shadow over these days, which may indeed be my last, or my worst. Of course, doctors told my mother I would not live past twelve or fifteen. In another week, I will be fifty,

so ...

11 May 1993

Today I am waiting on a call from the transplant coordinator about yesterday's tests, the initial steps in considering a double-lung transplant. What am I *doing*? All I know is that my doctor told me recently that he has talked to a transplant surgeon about me. I know that (1) he must feel it is time for this, that I cannot survive much longer the way I am; (2) I am going to have to confront reality and make some very difficult decisions that will be left solely up to me; (3) no matter what I do, the choices are not good ones. I cannot wait a long time to decide or I will be too sick for a transplant.

The surgery is new (ten years old) and the survivors are few. I wish I felt stronger. They told me the will to live is the key thing. There are many ways the deal can go wrong. I feel so confused. One part of me says, "*No, no, no.*" Another part says, "*Take the chance.*" I feel, in fact, that my doctor probably believes that if anyone can survive this, I can. A few years ago, I would have had this belief in myself, but I was not sick enough then. Now that I *am* sick enough, my faith in myself and in my strength is shaken. All I can do is proceed one step and one day at a time. I could be ruled out by the preliminary testing. Now is not the time to worry about the results of the surgery.

25 May 1993

Tonight I saw a repeat of an interview with James Brady, who made a long, slow physical comeback after being shot and losing much of his motor function. He said, "Never count yourself out. You have to keep trying and trying no matter how difficult life is." I sometimes try, especially now with this transplant decision hanging over me, to look at how other people in trouble are dealing with their lives. The Crisis Center also helps me to look beyond my own problems and I realize how fortunate I am still to be able to do work for them. In all their turmoil, the people I talk to have no idea they are my lifeline.

28 May 1993

I got the most beautiful letter from one of my nieces today. Just when I'm feeling so bad about my current situation. These letters are symbolic of the relationships themselves, and I value them as I once valued "love letters." Kept here, they remind me, whenever I need to be reminded, to treasure these younger people in my life whom I watched mature and who are just now becoming adults. I have kept their childhood drawings in my desk, and some I had framed and displayed until my workroom walls were covered. On my darkest days, I take out my letters, or take out one or two, and read them as I think of the quilts I want to make for these nieces. I think I will begin keeping a separate folder and sketches and ideas for each of their quilts. If I do not actually get them all made, at least they will see what I intended.

30 May 1993

I cannot seem to get much work done on the desert quilt. I am up all night on the Crisis line tonight and it is not busy, but the quilting is so involved—I must balance the frame on my lap with one hand over, and the other under, wearing thimbles—that it is difficult to get loose fast enough when the phone rings. The quilting itself is tiring now and I am more aware of the physical strength it takes.

3 June 1993

I have designated May as "Transplant Month." With too many choices and not enough certainties, I talked it over with myself and other people until I could not stand to anymore. And yet it is June and still going on. On Monday I have an appointment to talk to a psychologist.

The psychologist called me today; the priest called me yesterday. All I need now is a Buddhist monk and a rabbi. Frankly, if I knew how to contact either and thought they could offer help, I probably would try to talk to them, too. But in the end, it is up to me. I have to take the risk or the opportunity. I wish I felt better or strong enough to take such a step. They say I must want to live more than anything (they being the Transplant Team). I don't want to live on and on, sick and helpless, until everyone wishes I were gone. What *do* I want? I want to walk out the front door and get in the car and drive *anywhere*. I want to walk into a movie or a restaurant the way I used to. I have countless "wants," but I *don't* want to go through months of hell after a transplant goes bad or after it is too late to have a choice. Whoever said life was fair? Nobody I know of.

5 June 1993

Last night while working on the desert quilt, I noticed the drybrushed paint on the crane is too thick in places. Oh, I knew this before, but I hoped I was being too critical of my work. So I have begun the long, slow, arduous process of repairing this. Acrylic paint cannot be removed, once it is dry. I remember an art teacher talking about how oil paint's molecular structure can be broken down with paint thinners, while acrylic—being "something else"—cannot be thinned this way. I tried everything—scraping, covering, blending—

but it just got worse. Finally, at 3 a.m., I found myself punching tiny holes through the weave of the fabric over and over until the acrylic began to rough up, or flake, a little. Then I used an emery board, *very* cautiously, to sand off the flakes. It worked! But what a tedious process, and there is still more to do. At least I will feel better about the end result though. I want this quilt to be *right*.

6 June 1993

I have this fantasy. My last four *Symphony* quilts will be hung in a small space. My niece will play selected music to evoke Alice Walker's words from her essay "In Search of Our Mothers' Gardens": "Their striving spirits sought to rise, like frail whirlwinds from the hard red clay. And when those frail whirlwinds fell, in scattered particles, upon the ground, no one mourned. Instead, men lit candles to celebrate the emptiness that remained, as people do who enter a beautiful but vacant space." The audience will remember that the artist was striving to find both herself and a God of love.

22 June 1993

I canceled my Monday appointment at the transplant center Saturday night because I felt I just could not summon the effort to do the walking it would take to get there. Monday I was much better, and we are wondering if it can possibly be the new allergy-free air filter Eddie put in the air-conditioning and heating system.

23 June 1993

Last night for a while I began to have trouble again. I talked to myself a lot and even imagined a great spirit encircling me in its arms, and I am comforted by the knowledge that *I was better*, and so I will not be afraid.

I simply have to stay as calm as I can, and do whatever I can still do, and trust in the arms I can feel around me now. Fear is my *least* useful emotion. Love is my *most* useful emotion.

Crane detail from Georgia on My Mind, *with feathers replacing the paint*

28 June 1993

My latest *Forum* magazine is about "The Human Genome Project." I am interested, of course, because it's thought that genetic therapy might be used to treat cystic fibrosis. But after I read it, I see that its most significant observation is that here, as in other research, "knowledge precedes the ability to intervene." So someday it may help someone else, if not me, and this is good. Much better, I think, than double-lung transplants. The double-lung transplant cost is over $250,000, so researchers know they must increase their efforts on the genetic frontier.

29–30 June 1993

This weekend will be the Fourth of July and the beginning of Eddie's vacation. Today I read an article about Independence Day in which the writer quoted the words of Emma Lazarus at the base of the Statue of Liberty: "*Give me your tired, your poor, / Your huddled masses yearning to breathe free."* As a child, I not only read about immigrants coming to this country, but actually knew some who lived on my grandmother's street. Most of them were her age, grandparents living with their children and their grandchildren. I remember regarding these people with awe, feeling that they must be special to have come such a long way, perhaps enduring great hardships, to live in my country. (Only later did I find out about my own immigrant relatives, who died before I was born.) I was not supposed to go into anyone's home without telling my grandmother, but of course I did, and I loved listening to the Greek and Italian grandparents talk to their more American relatives in languages I could not understand. One of the blessings of childhood, I think, is that, having not yet acquired the habits of prejudice, the young can still experience the essence of the American ideal.

2 July 1993

Tonight I was watching a show on TV about some Vietnamese children who had been brought up here, and then as adults went back to Vietnam. Their family were Montagnards, the people who "lived in the hills," good and gentle people who never harmed anyone and yet were devastated by the war. I was struck by how healthy, strong, and confident the two Vietnamese-Americans were compared to the family they found back home. The parents and several siblings, looking haggard, half-starved, and broken, showed the ravages of war in their eyes. It was such a sad reunion that I was in tears before I knew it, shedding all those I've held back because, with my breathing problems, they practically choke me to death. My parents and grandparents always said, "You don't know how lucky you are," and how right they were! None of us knows until we can see the world through older eyes. As upset as I get at times with our system, I know we have great advantages and can make it better, especially now with women having more voice.

Mid-July 1993

I have been making tracings of all kinds of small symbols that I might quilt in the small squares when my *Symphony* series is done. I have made a grid to scale of my finished quilts. The small blocks in the quilt will be one and one-half inches square, so these are small tracings.

There was a time when I could quickly draw off these little tracings, but my hand is so unsteady I could hardly keep the curves straight. Little moons and spirals, stars, and, of course, the butterfly. I even found a circular, stylized butterfly (from Japan, ca. 1150).

[In mid-July Pat told me that she had taken another turn for the worse and would try to be put on the transplant list. The doctors, she said, had been pushing her to get on before it became too late, though there was no guarantee that she would survive or end up with a better life.]

24 July 1993

I have been talking with a priest from our parish. With things as they are, I began to feel I needed the comfort of my childhood religion, the *only* religion I have ever had. I was surprised, really, to find it is so easy to ask and accept forgiveness for a lifetime of painful separation, and to be able to take Communion weekly from now on here in my home. I still do not know why I have survived so long with this illness, but it has given me this late chance to reconcile my present life with my past. And something inside my head or my heart or my soul said, "*Do this*," and I have felt more at peace ever since.

I told my uncle because I knew he cared about me and my relationship to the church. He is also my godfather, in the old-fashioned sense of the word, and I knew he would be relieved when he heard.

Until now, my prayers—if the agonizing inside me could be called prayers—have been for all the wrong things. I prayed for relief, help,

Small tracings of symbols for Symphony *series*

some kind of miracle that would leave me cured and whole, as I never really have been. But now I am learning to pray for the strength to cope with the days ahead, whatever happens. If I have new lungs, the price will be high; in this gamble, the odds are against me. If I don't have the transplant, my days are numbered, but then, they always have been. Now I am trying to focus more on what I *can* do, can get done on a daily basis—and yet I feel less driven. It doesn't make much sense as I read it written down here, but the priest said something that puts my experience in a different light now. He said that people who suffer a great deal are really closest to God; as God sent His Son to suffer for the sins of all human beings, all who suffer join in this suffering of Christ, and in their struggle, they can be closer to God than those whose lives are relatively peaceful. I am trying to believe this now, but it is not easy.

2 August 1993

Our lives, Eddie's life and mine, took a bad turn as July ended. It was the hottest on record for days on end with temperatures in the high nineties. Even the nights were hot; our air conditioner saw us through this. But Eddie developed a kidney stone and was taken to the emergency room from work. The woman who drove him called me, and she didn't know what was wrong but said he was very sick. She thought it might be a heart attack. With this call, my whole life changed in an instant. I have no wish to write about this blow by blow, but two ER visits and one doctor visit later, I am trying to be the caregiver now. We have argued, of course, but now I know how devastated I would be without him—not without his physical support, not without his financial support, but without *him*. I thought about his voice saying, "I'm home," when he gets off in the afternoon, and his comforting presence when I am having trouble breathing at night, and his spoiling the dogs with treats, and his surprising me at Christmas with a little diamond heart necklace that hardly seemed a gift for someone wearing an oxygen tube. I thought about all we have been, and haven't been, to each other. How he operates from a gut level—"what you see is what you get"—while I over-analyze, weigh all the odds, and make lists. I worry, while he always says, "It'll be all right, it always has." These last few days I have worried and wondered how I could ever have managed—no, *lived*—without him. Suddenly the uncut grass, the painting left undone, and the hammock not put together don't seem to matter because he is still alive.

14 August 1993

I haven't written anything for almost two weeks. Eddie is okay now. I have decided to put aside the transplant idea, though I may look into the new DNA drug. I am also going to plan a trip, something I have been afraid of doing. Now I know it is the fear, more than my condition, that ties me here. If we have to get a van or mobile home, we will, but I want to enjoy the time I have as long as I can.

27 August 1993

I am still finishing the desert quilt and am also working on a strip-pieced quilt, and Mother has put Anna's *Cats* quilt together. I have ordered kits for the rest of the nieces. I want them all to have quilts, but I know I will never be able to finish the work I have started and five new quilts besides.

6 September 1993

I have been feeling better for a long time, maybe two months or close to it. In my typical way, I had been taking the credit for this, just assuming that I had prayed or analyzed my way into this improvement, that I had figured out how to manage the fear and the illness itself. Not until today did I realize that it had little to do with me and was just a gift, so unexpected that I did not recognize it.

6 October 1993

I am hospitalized, very sick, very tired. Eddie and my mother are staying with me. I cannot breathe well enough even to go to the bathroom alone. My hair is clean, but I haven't been able to comb it for three days. What toothbrush? I am praying a lot. I feel bad for Eddie and Mother for putting them through this terrible situation. I feel bad because, for the first time, I am clinging and afraid that I will stop breathing. Each breath is measured. I did everything I could think of to manage at home. I even put instructions for myself on a bottle of my inhaler, but suddenly, almost overnight, I became too ill to eat, to get to the bathroom, to think straight. Finally, I just told Mother, who had come over to keep me company, that I had to get some help. I called my doctor and we called Eddie at work so he could come home. I was in the middle of redoing the kitchen chairs and had added some shelves in the kitchen and done other things to distract me instead of acknowledging I was in serious trouble. Now I am back at square one.

23/24 October 1993

Today is 23/24, Saturday/Sunday, October. At least this is what a calendar at the foot of my bed says. The wall clock beside it says 11:05 p.m. I am in the *subacute* care unit of Baptist Hospital, in *critical care*. But what does this mean? I am someone to watch closely but not a regular floor patient. I do not think I have ever been this sick and do not know why, in God's name, I am still here and breathing.

25 October 1993

Midnight. Today I called my sister Katie, and asked Mother to call Cynthia. I needed them now, as never before. I feel as if I could draw strength somehow from them to get through this.

26 October 1993

Last night Katie and Anna came to the hospital. I wanted them to know how much I love them. Then Cynthia called and came to the hospital while they were still here. I felt so bad that each of them came about the same time. It was confusing. Anna was with Katie, and while I was able to say things I wanted to share with all of them, I still want to be sure Katie *knows* how important she has been in my life from the time I cut her toe off on the back of my bicycle until this moment.

I have very little lung capacity left. *Where* do I go from here?

[Pat's doctors had told her that morning that with only twenty percent of her lungs still functioning, they could give her no more than a year to live. She herself seemed to feel she had less than that, and yet when I got to the hospital, I found her still fighting for life.

She pleaded with us to tell her why she could not just relax and die. Her sister Jodie piped up, "Well, Patsy, I guess it's because you have all those quilts to finish up first." An inspired reply when all that we could know was that it was not time, that she was not ready.]

27 October 1993

My chest does not move when I breathe. This is frightening. Okay. Just worry instead about how to tell Katie that she is and has been more important to my life than she will ever know. *Finally* I work on my quilt. I think I will add feathers to the crane to straighten it out since the acrylic paint has no chance of being salvaged.

30 October 1993

I will now need some kind of home care since I have "progressed" to the point of total dependence on others for just about everything. I accept this and know I am lucky to have the insurance, and family who care, and a husband who is seeing me through this sickness. It will be more difficult to find meaning in these days ahead, but they *will* have meaning.

1 November 1993

Today Eddie called and said, "They are bringing a hospital bed to the house today. What do you want me to do?" I thought, "What *do* I want him to do? Listen to me when I talk to him? Lessen the pain of losing my last vestige of self-sufficiency? Say it will all be okay with these changes that will forever change my breathing treatment (*a little Gertrude Stein*) and change our lives together?"

Later. He has help coming getting the couch out; the garbage men will pick it up. We should have done this long ago. Bed will be in the den. I will have a commode chair. The doctor has ordered anything that will help. This scares me a little. Does it mean I can't walk? I have already tested myself. At first my legs seemed like someone else's, but now I can walk around the room. No physical therapist has yet come to my room, as before, to walk with me, and when I have asked about this, no one really has answered me. So I will revert to my old techniques, to my self-care program. My doctor comes in around noon. I have been reading and writing, off and on, all morning and afternoon. He says he will discharge me to go home as soon as all the home services are in place. Hurry and wait. The bed and commode are there. I am going to try to make Eddie's pot of coffee each day, as I have always done. It will be a thread of continuity connecting our previous life to this newest stage. (It will be good to write on a stable surface again.)

The hospital coordinator for Trinity HealthCare says it will be providing a nurse every day, a physical therapist twice a week, and a social worker to evaluate my needs. Even if I wake up afraid at night, I will have someone I can call. Is this a new trend in home care or is this only new to me? Twenty years ago, when I was first sent to a rehabilitation program, this broad, holistic approach was the latest thing. Rehab meant physical therapy, occupational therapy, and psychological counseling. Of course there were some *holes* in holistic, and bridging the gap between needs and wants and reality was difficult. But I did come away with a better image of myself and a desire to accomplish something. So I went to college and studied art; then I made quilts, large and small, and *dared* to call them art. Some wonderful people I hardly knew helped me have a show with my quilts. Somewhere in there my health began to fail again, but it hardly mattered because I had done so much more than I ever believed possible. One thing just led to another so perfectly, so beautifully, that I began to feel a little as if I didn't really deserve the praise and attention I got. I felt I needed to push myself to accomplish even more.

In the end, of course, I began having to spend time in the hospital, getting a little worse as the hospitalizations became more frequent.

8 p.m. Tonight I will finish this summary I have been writing as the "hospital people"—the nurses, respiratory therapists, aides, and orderlies—come in and out of my room. My nerves are much more frayed than they were yesterday. Is it because I am now aware as never before that I am going home in a metaphorical sense as well as a literal one? I am approaching the end of my life on this planet. When I used to talk about death, it was somewhere out there in the distance, never this close. Talking about it was even a way of holding it back. But now as the end approaches, I must face the fact and make decisions. I am writing down information for Eddie about the bills, the bank, and so forth. I also want my mother to *know* I love her before I leave. I see this as important now. *All* my family are important now—they always have been.

Finally, something I read in a paper from the church has been on my mind: "*We can hug our pain to ourselves. We can turn inward and nurture resentment, envy, and pure misery. Or we can let our suffering soften us. It can teach us compassion for all who suffer.*" I worry that at times I have hugged my pain to myself, but certainly this last trip to the hospital exposed me with my sickness for all to see. None of my family, aside from Eddie, actually realized the volume of secretions from my lungs I deal with daily. Maybe there was no need to have them witness this, but now they know. Now my family sees how sick and helpless I am, dying by inches, how much I cough, how hard it is for me to breathe. I sense they are astounded and wonder how I can live like this. Sometimes I can hardly believe it myself.

These jottings have helped me get through this time in the hospital before I go home to my bed in the den tomorrow. My mother and husband bought new sheets for it and have things looking good for my homecoming, my husband says. I can't imagine them shopping together, but it is probably good for them to help each other now. I hope with all my heart I can do tomorrow with some quiet dignity. *Please let me not be bitchy because I have lost this last bit of control over my life. I will be okay with this.* I will be with Eddie and FuFu again at last. At last.

2 November 1993

I am waiting for Eddie to get off work and to come here to take me home, and waiting to see what the insurance and home care and medical "folks" will work out. Normally, I would be dressed and sitting in a chair waiting, but at this time, I am still in a gown in bed. I almost decided to try to get dressed, but the finding of street wear required too much exertion. Okay, I also have noticed some mental problems I can't put my finger on. Is this temporary? It took me all morning to try to balance the checkbook; my writing is not right, but what is wrong? *Please let me function as well as I can function.*

3:15 p.m. So far I have heard from no one. I refuse, on this one day, to call and check. It is my day to let everyone else take care of things, as they have told me to. I wonder if the new bed, the health care professionals, my husband, and my family will all be out there in our home and someone will say, "Where's Patsy?" No, they won't. Something is wrong.

4:15 p.m. My husband calls and says he is on the way with oxygen. He has talked to no one. I suggest he call Trinity HealthCare. They say there is a *snag*; the insurance provider does not want to cover this home care. So, I have in my home a husband, a dog, a hospital bed, and a commode chair. The house has been cleaned up for us. My mother has made us soup and dessert for tonight.

5 p.m. My God, I sometimes am amazed at how I continue to believe that things will work out. I actually sat here all day thinking everything was being taken care of. My doctor came in just now. He says he can't release me to go home without someone there, given my present condition. He is trying to get the insurance people to see that home care is cheaper and better for me than the hospital. Good luck. I feel even more anxious now. What a day.

3 November 1993

8 a.m. Another day in paradise.

Today *I am working on my quilt.* Last night the respiratory therapist told me that there is a note on my chart to have the rehab therapist talk to me about moving to the rehab floor, 9 or 18. I may be moving today so I can stay in the hospital.

9 a.m. The quilt is in the corner of my room. Sheets and towels from the last two days are piled up in the two room chairs. Water from Sunday's bath is still in the sink. I am getting up and going to the bathroom by myself now. This is something I found out that I can do on my own by not following orders to call the desk for help. Life is still a series of problems that must be worked out. *Life* is the key word here.

4 November 1993

10 a.m. What an emotional trip I have already had today for someone who hasn't left her bed! I was still in a half-sleep, trying to keep my anxiety from creeping in, when I suddenly woke up to find a woman standing here looking at me. She says she is a social worker with the "skilled nursing care" facility and she asks if we can afford to pay for nursing care three or four days or hours, I don't remember which. Later my doctor himself comes in and says *nobody* can afford any of this nursing care. I tried to call Trinity HealthCare myself, but as if things were not already confused enough, my sinus trouble flared up, so I could not hear anything but the air *swooshing* loudly in my head.

Late morning. I called my sister Katie and asked if she could help get this worked out today. Katie comes in, early afternoon, and talks to the home care coordinator, who is about to leave for a conference. Katie comes back and says the woman has promised to get back with us by late afternoon. Katie stays until around 5:30 p.m. Eddie comes in before she leaves. My doctor also comes by to say he is still working on home support for me. We never do hear from the health care coordinator.

Later. Around midnight, a respiratory therapist came in for my last treatment and we started talking. I found myself spilling out all my frustration and pain. I could not believe what I was doing. Even more amazing, she lovingly put her arm around me. I could not believe this was happening. Two days ago, I refused another IV catheter being put in. They had run out of places and veins and had even tried my shoulder. *No,* I said, *no, no, no.* They went and got an order to quit the IV.

I always say I can do whatever I have to do, and I am certain that I can do so this time. The insurance company has not budged and will only pay for skilled nursing care, so I expect I will end up in that facility. Last night Eddie went to the ninth floor to check it out and said it looks much like this floor. While it is not what I would choose, it will be all right once I settle in, and maybe then I can work on my quilts. I am not having much luck now and feel very unsettled.

5 November 1993

This was the worst day yet. At noon, with the weekend looming ahead, there was still no word from *anybody.* So I finally took some steps myself. I just couldn't *sit here* any longer. I guess this was a mistake; Eddie seems to think it was. But then why do I feel so much better?

I myself called the home care coordinator. She said she is working on a proposal for our insurance company and will let me know when she knows what is going to happen. The exact same story I've heard every day this week.

7 November 1993

I feel about 100 percent better. My niece Julie spent some time here Saturday and Sunday afternoons, and just having her close was so comforting. Even if she just sits quietly, it takes away the weekend loneliness of being in the hospital. She brought me fall leaves and chocolate. I feel so elated. What a perfect gift!

8 November 1993

I am supposed to be walking a little with my oxygen so my status can be evaluated. Well, today as I walked in the hall, doing a good deal better than I thought I would, I suddenly felt like running just for the heck of it. In my mind, I raced down the hall, got into the elevator, ran through the lobby and out the front door, and down the street toward home. It was just like a sexual fantasy, which leaves out what you don't care about and enhances what you do care about. My God, did it really take just a short walk in the hall for this "sexual fantasy" to kick in?! (Well, I did say *fantasy*.)

Otherwise, this Monday was a lost day, emotionally and—emotionally. My doctor came in with bad news. My insurance company won't pay.

13 November 1993

Saturday afternoon. Late Friday, two women who are with Baptist Hospital came to my room and *very sweetly* said my insurance will not cover last week's hospitalization, but they want me to let them move me on Monday to the hospital's skilled nursing unit, which I happen to know is at least as expensive as this. Did they really think I would just as sweetly cooperate with the insurance people, who have ruled out the home nursing that would be best? It has all been the most unethical, cruel, and heartless thing that has ever happened to me.

Since then, I have been using every spare minute to get down on paper a record of what has been done in this case, and in writing it out, I have discovered a loophole the insurance people created for themselves. So here I am, anxious and insecure about whether I will be able to go home for the holidays. I am going to take a nap, an unusual thing for me to do. Maybe it will improve my state of mind.

16 November 1993

Maybe it didn't. I thought a long time about writing a lot more about the insurance snafu in here, but it has already consumed my life for an entire week. It just got my adrenaline going, and then, in the middle of it, I suddenly realized I was no longer angry or fearful as much as energized because I had found a *cause* that for these two days gave my life a *purpose*. By yesterday, I felt ready to drop the issue, to admit I was wrong for getting upset with everyone while enjoying the knowledge that I had surprised the people who thought me incapable of fighting the system. I apologized Wednesday and came to my new room, 915 in the skilled nursing facility. Thanksgiving is next week. I will try once again to finish the desert quilt and *maybe* get home.

20 November 1993

Saturday. *One* day at a time. There are six days until Thanksgiving. If I *never* see another piece of this paper tape from the IV, which has removed every hair from my arms now, it will be too soon. I have also been having a terrible time with the heat. They keep it very warm in this unit because there are so many old people here. When the temperature dropped to the thirties, the heat came on in full force. My two fans were not enough to offset it, and most of the nurses on the floor did not seem to understand my *need* for *cold air*. Luckily one or two did, and I am sure one of them called for a maintenance man. He was my last hope and he saved me from another hour of desperation. He said *he* has some breathing problems himself and can't sleep or breathe in a room over sixty degrees at night, and he was able to turn up the air and cut off the heat. Everyone up to this point had said nothing could be done, and yet now it is cool. I slept restfully in the coolness last night; I savored the air and feel well compared to last week. I hope my doctor *will* let me go home for Thanksgiving.

[Released as hoped just before the holiday, Pat was grateful to be heading home, even though she now had a huge hospital bill her insurance company said it was not bound to pay by the terms of her policy. The Clines began an appeal of this action immediately.]

1 December 1993

The last month in 1993. No, I did not get the desert quilt finished. It is sitting right here on my hospital bed in the den of my home. Not much is left to be done, but I was disappointed in myself. Now I have to hire a sitter this week, or next, someone to stay with me. I am dreading this little maneuver, but once I have it behind me, I will get back to work full speed on my quilts.

Before I lay to rest this last hospitalization, I did want to put something more in here about an incident that touched me deeply.

It goes back to November 4, 1993, late Wednesday night, when one of the several respiratory therapists who came to my room lent an ear as I unloaded about the insurance situation and my life. Everything was so pent up inside me, I babbled, running on and on. As a rule, I would never do this, not even with friends and relatives, much less with medical staff. It is easier for me to write than to talk about personal problems, and sometimes, of course, I cannot do either one.

But this time I did, and suddenly she was putting her arm around me. Then after a while, she told me about her little boy, six years old. His school had called her in recently and told her that he was having some problems. In trying to get the advice of some doctors and psychiatrists, she had seen the kind of red tape and slow, confused process that I was fuming about. She agreed that the system is going bad. Everyone seems to have hired someone else to eliminate paperwork and look out for their special interests. This has only resulted in more red tape and no real concern for the people involved, not for the patients and not for the staff like herself.

I want to remember her always. The unexpected kindness of strangers affects me as deeply—no, more—than the system's cruel lack of concern.

3 December 1993

I was hospitalized for *seven* weeks, and I thought I would *never* be okay again. But now I am planning for Christmas! I want to do something special for Eddie and want to enjoy and appreciate being alive another year. I have come such a long way. I have a hospital bed and commode chair, prescriptions for every conceivable pain—well, not really, but five or six at least, including an antidepressant. Though this could never be said aloud, I think my doctor was telling me as I left, "If you want to make your exit at home, these medications will give you that option. But if you come back to me and go in the hospital, I will have to do everything I can to keep you alive." But then, it is always a bad idea to try to second-guess someone. I can only live as I have in the past, a *day* at a time. The drugs are tucked away in a drawer for now. I may never use them.

In any case, for some reason I don't understand, life seems much more valuable now than ever before, maybe because I know it is almost over. I want to give Eddie these few precious days and make them as good as I can for him. Of all the onlookers, he has had to carry the most emotional pain. The others have also suffered, but they have not had to *live* with me, or go to sleep beside me, or wake up with me sitting up in my sleep beside them. I want to do his family album for Christmas and am going to work very hard at this.

17 December 1993

Almost Christmas. Still no sitter. My breathing has gotten a little worse, and it has seemed too much trouble to interview anyone. Mother is going to help here Christmas. I think I can get through it. I have decided to stay home to die. I don't want to be in the cold, sterile atmosphere of a hospital. I don't want to be put on a respirator, or even a ventilator. But what *do* I want?

20 December 1993

I am *still* finishing Richard and Carol's quilt. My slow pace now is a testament to my life. October and November were lost weeks in the hospital. I was the sickest I have ever been. I felt as if I could not stand to live any longer, but I *could not* die. One part of me clung to the unfinished segment of my life, while the other part prayed that I could let it go. The unfinished part won out, though I could not even stand or walk alone after the bout with pneumonia.

Today I am making cookies for Christmas gifts. It is now difficult to stand or walk any distance, and I imagine this will be the last time I can do this. So I am also going to make dressing for Christmas: the *works*! And I am going to savor every moment. Merry Christmas! It truly does feel great to be alive, to be able to appreciate my life as long as I have it.

4 January 1994

Here I am at 2 a.m., trying to pull myself together for another new year of living in the moment. I am asking myself, "What do I do now?" I want to spend a lot of time on my quilts. Eddie and I have both been under the weather with some kind of sinus thing. We've been alternating between our short tempers and sympathy. He believes in just letting things go, while I am afraid of getting so far behind, I will never catch up. We are dealing with monumental problems like taking the Christmas decorations down, catching up on laundry, and emptying out the leftovers in the refrigerator. The boxed-up Christmas candles and cards are piled up waiting to be stored away. I decided to go a lot easier on Christmas several years ago. Before that, we had always had a big tree my husband cut down himself, and compared to the old routine, we did things very simply this year. Still there is always that hangover from the holidays.

But I need to be writing instead of how grateful I am to have had this additional Christmas with people I care about. I *am* grateful. Today I received a book of postcards of work by women artists from Meg. I love to hear from this niece because she is so flip and funny and irreverent. I guess I remember being that way myself, and it added a lighthearted touch this afternoon. I need to wake up tomorrow on this note and clean up and clear off this hospital bed that looks like a yard sale. I should be getting talking-book cassettes soon, so I will listen and sew, and finish some things, and at least begin my series.

6 January 1994

I do not believe there is ever work without hope. The very act of working is tied to having a goal and must be about hope, whether it is the factory work of a woman to support a child, or the work of a world-famous artist, or the piecing together of fabrics by someone as unknown as I am.

4 February 1994

I am getting a sitter next week. A nurse came by today. This should help me to stay at home and get back to work on my quilts.

8 February 1994

Today I set up my quilt in my hospital bed so my back and the chest pain are relieved enough to work. The visiting nurse has worked out well. The sitter, not so well. Yesterday when the woman came by, I had nothing for her to do. The house had been cleaned the day before and there was no need to cook. I suggested maybe she could just "sit," since I was better than when I engaged her. She said she couldn't just sit; she *had to work*, which I could appreciate. So I let her go home. She told me she had worked all night and was very tired. I think she is coming by one more time to see if she can do anything. Then I can cancel and later get back on home health care as my needs require.

9 February 1994

Cynthia called today. It was good to hear from her. And now I am writing to tell her more about my newest idea. All I had to do was take a photo with the shades of color over a grid and explain what is there. This has a way of making me *think* and making me use my time to good purpose. I cannot let the fact that I am now in pain with my lungs stop me here. My pain does not seem to be getting any worse, so maybe this is not a crisis, but just a stage. (Am I crazy?)

If I could get through an abscessed tooth as I did, I am sure I can get through anything painful. In my home health folder I found a dentist who works in the patient's home; I also found a beautician. Maybe I can get my hair and teeth worked on after all.

Listening to the books on tape now is wonderful. I wish I had done this long ago. I will order some of the classics next. It is *perfect* when I am quilting once I get past the difficult parts.

17 February 1994

Today more chest pain began on my right, lower side. It is very painful on moving. The left side seems to hurt a little too. Well, what do I do now? How do I handle this? Is this *it?* I was given some pills for pain when I left the hospital, but I don't want to waste them or use them too freely. I divided one in half and took it. It hasn't helped much at all. Mostly, I have tried to sit still, but that is only possible for so long.

26 February 1994

I have heard it said that great pain produces great art. Emotional maybe, but physical? Pain plays tricks with my mind and I am very distracted. I don't know if it is the pain or the painkiller.

1 March 1994

Julie has spent the week with us. She needed to work on a paper for school that is due after break. It has been so nice having her around the house. Mother brought us supper tonight. FuFu is getting used to company, with all the health care workers and relatives coming in and out.

Pat with her niece Julie Meiman at the Meristem opening, March 1991

5 March 1994

Watching television this weekend, I caught a program about Japanese weavers and makers of indigo cloth. These artisans create special pieces to live on after they die and impart to the next generation what their creators' lives had to teach posterity. Is this possible, or does each generation have to find its own way? Another hard question.

22 March 1994

Exactly three years from the opening of my quilt show. It was during Women's History Month. To mark the day, I sent Meristem a donation to forward to Camp Sister Spirit, a woman's retreat down in Mississippi. I read about it recently in my National Organization for Women newsletter. (I am a very fringe member of NOW.)

I found the old photo that I have attached to the front of this journal while I was throwing away a bunch of outdated stuff in my wallet. It was taken for an ID card,  long expired. When I looked at it, I realized it was taken in October 1990, while I was still able to get out a little: the October before my quilts were hung at Meristem, the October after this journal began, about halfway between these two efforts—my writing and sewing— that share the good, human side of my life. I am afraid if anyone sees me today, the outward person I was is gone, lost to plastic tubes and bluish complexion and hair that is sometimes uncombed because even this is too hard to manage.

25 March 1994

Instruction

My hands that guide a needle
In their turn are led
Relentlessly and deftly
As a needle leads a thread
Other hands are teaching
My needle: When I sew
I feel the cool, thin fingers
Of hands I do not know.
They urge my needle onward,
They smooth my seams, until
The worry of my stitches

Smothers in their skill.
All the tired women
Who sewed their lives away,
Speak in my deft fingers
As I sew today.
—Hazel Hall (1886–1924)

I am trying to write while I feel better. Sometimes I think I write only when I feel troubled, or sick, or both. When I am well and my thinking is better, I work; I catch up. And since I *am* breathing better, I am working on my quilts again and feel more hopeful, if not for myself, for my quilts. Later, I want to be able to look at this page and see that I could feel this good after being so ill. Then I will not be able to say, "I cannot go through this." I will know that I can.

I am so sorry about my journal getting wet. I spilled a large glass of water in my bed and it went all over everything. What a day that was. Today is better.

26 March 1994

I believe that when a doctor says, "You only have X years at the most. We have done everything we can do," you begin to try to make your life count in some way in this intervening time. When you live past the experts' estimates, you are a *miracle* in a way, or you could be a *miscalculation*, a *drain* on the insurance company, a *burden* to those who love you, or a *statistic* (.003 people out of every 100,000 live beyond the expected death with this disease). Well, I choose to be a *miracle*, and I have something of importance that I have been doing with this extra time. Now my life is not just about pain or suffering. Or *is* it? What would I be doing if I were well? I cannot even imagine that anymore. And anyway, the truth is the truth: no one is happier or feels better than I do when Eddie hugs me (he often comes up behind me and kisses my hair or neck and gives me a hug), or when my dog lies beside me with his head on my arm as we drift off to sleep, or when I finish a quilt and watch the recipient's face when I give it to her or to him. I must never forget how fortunate I am to feel loved and feel useful during this difficult time.

30 March 1994

I saw in the paper that one of my Crisis Center people, a frequent caller especially on the late night shift, was hit by a truck and killed. I was so upset. One of the other workers phoned me because, she said, I was about the only one he had not gotten angry at. I cannot say whether this is good or bad in this age of trendy psycho-speak and talk about co-dependency. I was told at one point by another volunteer that if we let this individual talk too long, it would be co-dependent behavior on our part. Well, I don't know. Personally, I saw it as having respect for another human being. I expect there is a lot of condescension among lots of therapists. I cannot help it; it is what I feel. This caller mentioned his brother often, so I know someone else kept in touch with him, came and got him for holidays, rescued him from the hospitals and jails, and must have loved him in spite of himself. But since he was mentally ill, this man never was able to feel whatever concern and affection others did have for him. I sent his brother a card (anonymously) and told him that my husband and I will miss J—. I am even more grateful now that I did take some time with him because I believed he wanted the same things all of us want: to feel genuine love and respect. I imagine he never felt either.

17 April 1994

Only a quick move of the pen; I have work to be done. Today I had family over for pizza and ice cream and cake. Three cakes! It is Mother's and Eddie's and my nephew Jimmy's birthday. Others had to do the physical work, but it went well.

I have been working on the ram's skull on the desert quilt, which involves a wide range of techniques: trapunto, strip piecing, appliqué, strip appliqués, stipple quilting, and the regular quilt stitch. I really am having a time with it. I realize I try to quilt like a painter; I do not work in one continuous line, but move around within the design to bring out the dimension of the skull, the movement of the clouds, the flight of the crane—qualities that give this quilt more than a static, flat surface.

I am so tired. My writing seems to reflect this, but I do want to keep my ideas and feelings here. I always think, for *future reference*, and yet I hardly ever reread anything. Sometimes I don't know what it is all about, this keeping of journals.

22 April 1994

At last, at last! Such a *good* day. First, the doctor's office called and acknowledged receiving its copy of the three-page letter I wrote as a final appeal to the insurance company. Until I wrote this letter, nobody understood what I was upset about (or they knew, but knew there was not much, if anything, any of us could do at the time). Now, as I proceed with filing all the available appeals—and Eddie says he is going to court if he has to because of what the hospital and insurance company did to us in our worst circumstances ever—I can see that things got worse as more and more people got involved: the OPM, PPO, EOB, and NALC (everybody and everything goes by initials these days). My letter's way of approaching the insurance company may have looked silly; it certainly was not businesslike. But all that had failed, so I simply reverted to something a little shameless. I sent with my letter some Polaroid photos and tried to tell the person who opened it *who* I am and what happened and why the situation was so unfair. I will put a copy of my letter here.

31 March 1994
U.S. Office of Personnel Management,
Insurance Review Division
To Whom It May Concern:

My "case" is spelled out in the attached papers, particularly in my doctor's letter. This doctor has treated me for a long time. There is little I can add now except that until now my husband and I felt that I was covered for catastrophic illness, which is certainly what has slowly taken place in my life. My physician, at the time of this discontinuance of benefits, said he "could not in good conscience" discharge me as sick as I was when the insurance PPO and hospital business office simultaneously decided I no longer needed to be hospitalized. People who never saw me struggling through this last hospitalization [suddenly] felt I was not in need of medical care of any kind ... because bills were piling up.

... I [have] decided, since you can't see me or meet me, to tell you who I am; not because I am somebody, but because I am everybody. This recent ... treatment by the hospital and by the insurance company made me feel like a pariah, which I am not. I am a living, breathing (still, with assistance) human being. The first photo (#1, on the back) is of me in 1991, just as I began this final stage of my sickness. I used oxygen then, but not constantly. I am in the pink sweater and I am with a teacher/friend who helped bring about a "show" of my quilts. All the physical labor (hanging and labeling) was done by college friends who were aware of my situation. (I was hospitalized twice while preparing these quilts for the show.) Each piece had excerpts of my writing (from journals I have kept while working on my quilts). Each has now been given to [someone who] helped me survive with ... prayers and with ... love.

The second photo, #2, shows friends and family who came to the quilt show, as does #3. I thought perhaps I would seem more like someone you might know if you knew who I was. You can see that I have used the downtime, during the recent years with the more debilitating effects of lung disease, to create quilts and wall hangings for family and friends who have always been there for me.

Photos #4 and #5 show where and how I live now, spring 1994.

145

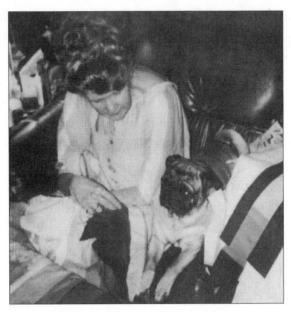

Pat with FuFu in her den, 1994

I have a hospital bed at home because I sleep sitting up, and a com-mode chair in our den. I dress as if I were going to a studio to work, but in truth I will never leave my home to go anywhere again until I die.

I have never smoked. My disease is genetic in origin. I cannot "do" anything about it. I can only try to survive the terrible bouts of infection and, of course, I will lose this fight one day. I believe that it is a human desire to want to live as long as my life has meaning. I feel that I am being penalized for being sick too long. Personally, I have cherished every moment I have had, deserved or not. Children die of this disease every day, but hopefully in the near future this won't happen any longer. It has been said that Medical Technology has gone way beyond the financial and social systems to back it up. I guess this is part of the problem. At first I believed the insurance company just did not understand the shape I was in, but now I believe it was more sinister than that. I think it did not matter what shape I was in; they wanted me out of the hospital regardless of what might happen to me if the hospital coerced me to leave.

At this time and in previous appeals, I only am asking for some justice [after] the way I have been treated and the stress it has put on my husband, who is already dealing with losing me. I would certainly rather be at home with my fat little dog and an ancient dog (photo #6) beside my bed. I can't draw comfort from them when I am in the hospital. My husband is here; my mother lives a few blocks away. It is hard on everybody when I am in the hospital and any time spent there is out of necessity. I only go as a last resort and this time I almost waited too late. I was admitted to the Pulmonary floor, then moved to the Critical Care Unit (because I became very ill), then moved back to the Pulmonary floor where recovery was slow because I had so many problems. Finally I was moved to the Skilled Nursing Facility (when rehab was refused) and my doctor felt Medicare would cover me there. It seems as though I got lost in the process, and now I owe approximately $12,000.

Sadly, it is all about money, ... not life—unless it is yours.
Sincerely,
Patricia R. Cline

[On May 28, in a short note, Pat told me she was still "having about as much trouble dying as living," but wanted to ask me to speak at her funeral "if and when" she was finally finished with her quilting "and able to fall asleep." "She feels she needs to be getting ready," I paraphrased in my journal after we spoke on the phone a few days later. "She's going to talk to a hospice program ... and has made an effort to mend her early Catholic connections to please her family."]

30 May 1994

I am only going to write a minute because I am working every moment I can on Richard and Carol's quilt. They will be here in two weeks for the wedding. I have been sick again lately, and this has slowed things down. When you realize you cannot breathe well enough to *quilt*, the jig is pretty much up, I guess.

Tonight I got such a lift from Natalie, who graduates this weekend from high school. The "baby" among the family's girls. (In five more years, Jon, the "male family baby," will end this generation of children.) It seems like only yesterday …

Tonight Natalie called to thank me for her graduation gift. She also sent me her annual to look at. When Eddie, who took the gift over, brought the book back and handed it to me, he said excitedly, "Hurry and look at this," pointing to the quotation Natalie had used for the caption under her picture:

Natalie Elaine Doan

Art has no race, creed, or gender, but is an expression of a human impulse.   —Aunt Patsy

Spanish Club 10-11; Senior Class Art Director; Camp Anytown 10; Renaissance 10; Art Show 10-11; Governor's School for the Arts 11; Scholastic Art Competition 12; Tennis 9.

I felt *so* proud of her for her achievements, but I wanted to laugh, or cry, because I could still see her running toward the ocean on that first trip to Florida, saying, "So much sand, so much sand." She was about three and finally just sat down in it. The ocean didn't particularly interest her. I remember how I loved to hug her, and how much joy she brought into our lives as a child. I really don't remember when or what I wrote her about art being a *human* impulse, not just a *male* impulse. I may even have been quoting someone else. It doesn't matter now. The other students quoted Shakespeare, Charles Dickens, the Bible. Hers was the one and only Aunt Patsy quote.

I do not believe anything could have touched me as much as this, considering the state I am in. She reminded me we had that artistic connection, that something special, even if we do hear a different drummer occasionally. This was her way of letting me know she loves me and remembers me beyond the life I have now. All this, as I write down the words as they tumble out, sounds so filled with self-importance, which is not what I feel. I feel gratitude, for she has made me remember that there were better days and that I mean something to *her*. I wonder what her teachers thought.

15 June 1994

I am back working at the Crisis Center from home. The earlier shift is working out well. I missed it after my last illness.

27 June 1994

I do feel guilty about this lovely book getting soaked. Since the water episode, I have also spilled a glass of milk here in bed, with all my books and things. Sometimes I just want to cry when I see that my life has come to this: my stuff and me all heaped up together in this efficiency, one-room den/hospital/studio. It's really rather funny how my setup here has evolved.

My sister Jodie called one day a week or so ago and persuaded me to talk to someone with Hospice. It sounds like a good alternative to a "ninth hour" hospitalization that could result in Eddie ending up with a large bill and no wife to show for it. Of course, everything is so complicated now, we cannot get a straight answer from our insurance on this. The doctor leaves it up to us as to whether we are ready to implement this type of care, and we ourselves are not sure we're ready.

I am in such a bad mood, I should not be writing tonight. I feel irritable and edgy. I've had one of those days where Eddie says, "It must be the full moon." He will be on vacation for two weeks beginning next Saturday. We had planned on having a trip instead of a lung transplant, but no trip now. We couldn't manage the volume of oxygen I require, for one thing, and my health is just too fragile. Eddie hasn't mentioned the trip we planned or any disappointment, or how hemmed in *he* must feel by our situation. It is such an overwhelming, painful feeling that goes through my heart to realize I have become his child—that is what it feels like—and a burden.

Katie and Mike brought over a video of Anna's wedding after the event. When I saw Eddie there at the reception in his new suit, looking so handsome, I realized I never see him this way anymore, "my nurse out of uniform." I think I even felt jealous, as ashamed as I am to admit this. *How could he dare enjoy himself at my niece's wedding without me?*

I will finish writing my shame here by saying I ordered two vacation tapes: "A Train Trip through Canada" and "An Alaskan Cruise." I have this idea that we can watch these one afternoon and sort of experience places we talked about going to one day. I had actually, a few years ago, sent off for information about the train ride through Canada. The odds are Eddie will not be thrilled at the idea of going on a vicarious vacation, but I am determined that we will enjoy this. I know that my substitute for the real thing may make what we're missing more painful. And I wish I knew the answer to the question, *"How do you live and how do you love when it is almost over, but not yet over?"* I need to quilt and think about this.

8 and 22 July 1994

I have to write out a story I need to remember and can refer to whenever I get to cursing the life I am forced to live now and start crying, *"Why me?"* It is enough to say I recently heard it with the profound understanding that none of us disabled or physically challenged people should take what we have for granted. Those of us lucky enough to have friends and family, and something to say about how we are going to live and die, should reach out to those who do not.

The Lynchburg Story

This true story took place at the hospital in Lynchburg, Virginia, and precisely what happened was this: the forced

sterilization of children and others considered *undesirable people.*
These *undesirables* included imbeciles, cripples, the blind and
deaf and deformed, epileptics, alcoholics, drug addicts, people
with tuberculosis or syphilis, the mentally ill or feeble-minded,
homosexuals, and anyone who was not "cost effective," meaning *any* residents of state prisons, mental hospitals, or other
such institutions.

Lynchburg's idea was to protect the racial purity of the fit-
test and save these privileged white people the expense of car-
ing for the *unfit.* Whatever justification the powers behind this
thought they had, 8,300 people were sterilized. In retrospect,
no one was proud of what happened. The nurses never talked
about it.

Hitler was meanwhile refining his own massive sterilization program, and ironically, after World War II, the Lynchburg
sterilizations did not stop but actually increased.

14 July 1994

I sent my brother, Richard, a long letter today with a list of my
favorite songs and music and books, as he asked me to do when he
wrote. It was nice to take this memory trip back through time
and far away from this room as I spent the afternoon playing all my
old tapes.

16 July 1994

Recently I heard Gloria Steinem say in a TV documentary, "If
the flap of a butterfly's wing can change the weather a hundred miles
away (and scientists now say it can), then the women who have
struggled and are still struggling for equality can certainly make a
difference." I have to believe and remember this.

20 July 1994

This week marks the 25th anniversary of the moon landing. It was around the time Eddie was injured and brought home from Vietnam, and around the time Martin Luther King, Jr., was shot. It seems like only yesterday.

23 July 1994

Eddie is having to help me bathe in the tub now. It feels like a line has been crossed. He was kind and very loving, but I felt so pathetic.

The 20th was the 25th anniversary of the moon landing. The 21st of this month was our 21st wedding anniversary. The moon is full this week.

My Eucharistic minister, Jean, is coming in the morning with Communion. I enjoy her visits. She is a comfortable person to be around.

26 July 1994

I am working hard to finish my quilting. Last night, for some reason, I wrote a note for Eddie about my rings, my family keepsakes, a christening dress (vintage 1943), a small child's glove that was my father's, a very old pair of glasses, my father's dog tags from WWII, my grandmother's wedding ring in a little rosary box of hers, and a few other things like this. I thought I should see what Eddie wants and leave the rest to Anne, the next-oldest sister, because I know she will be fair in giving them to my nieces and nephews and will be a good judge as to who might want which, if any, of these old keepsakes. I don't know why I felt a need to do this *now*, but I did.

1 August 1994

I have to take back my feelings about videos. I hate being in them on Christmas and Thanksgiving, but now they let me enjoy at least some of the family celebrations I can no longer attend. My niece Anna's wedding was such an experience. It looked so pretty and everyone worked so hard. I could not believe Mother made seven bridesmaids' dresses (with Katie's help). Now everything's settled down. She's the first niece to marry, and it doesn't seem possible that this is the little girl I can still see rocking in her little chair as we grown-ups dealt with the loss of her first baby sister. We were all rushing to take away the new baby's bed and little clothes and store them away before Katie left the hospital. Anna, three years old, just rocked and rocked, never saying anything. This image has somehow always stayed in my head, I believe, because I have seen a look on Anna's face from time to time—pensive and somehow distant—that has reminded me of that sad day so long ago.

Now someday she will be having children of her own.

8 August 1994

I have just about finished my desert quilt. I am sewing around the borders and preparing to fix my troubled crane. Perhaps I should say, as they do on the labels of hand-dyed fabrics and hand-loomed cloth, "The irregularities and imperfections are due to the fact that this was created by hand. As such, they enhance the product's overall effect." This is the first quilt I have finished during this stage of my illness. *Lung disease* always sounds sort of repulsive, but it was a fashionable malady with the "decadent" artists of earlier times, and now I have joined their company.

14 August 1994

I have been *very* ill since last Monday. Home health is doing IV antibiotics. What *is* very ill? *Very, very* ill? All day I had very consciously to breathe in and breathe out. I was more aware of it all because I did not have my usual strong bronchial dilators and anxiety drugs, but I think it was easier on those around me, and even on me, because I did not have the emotional swoops up and down that I get with that other medication.

Today I noticed my dog has developed what I think are sympathy symptoms, and Eddie had to take him to the vet. I read some. I watched TV some. I ate. I began to think, *What now?* I hugged Eddie and FuFu but how can you show enough love for someone who wanted a wife, but now has a helpless burden on his hands?

Carol, my brother Richard's wife (even as I just wrote out who Carol is I wondered why I do this all the time, as if I am *telling someone else* about my thoughts, but anyway), sent me three *Griffin and Sabine* books, and today I read all three. What a joy! Even in the midst of all this, another good day. Right in the eye of the storm, such a wonderful gift! I have got to write her as soon as I can.

19 August 1994

I have just read a poem by Alice Walker, "Each One, Pull One," and as usual, I am deeply moved by her words. "Even before we are dead," she writes, "they are busy / trying to bury us." And then, "Did we write exactly what we saw, / as clearly as we could? Were we unsophisticated / enough to cry and scream?"

18 September 1994

This week another turning point. I cannot take care of my most basic needs most of the time. It is so hard on Eddie, but I hope I can still stay home. Hospice is going to help us. We are trying to hire a sitter, someone to be here when Eddie is working. I am still trying to focus on the *good stuff*, to live *in the moment*. Richard is coming to get his quilt, so I'll know that he and Carol finally have it. My sister Anne and her husband, Greg, came up this weekend and are coming back next weekend. I sense that nobody knows what to do about me. I have told Eddie I will go to a nursing home if he wants to let go of the responsibility. He says no. What should I do? Tonight he said we will just take things a day at a time. I am so tired of *a day at a time*.

20 September 1994

We are trying to get Hospice in here to help, but it is so hard to work it out. I cannot believe how complicated it all is. We have to sign off our insurance and my Medicare and go on their Medicare. I am afraid of losing my oxygen benefits and the breathing medicine. In fact, I am more afraid than ever, and no one seems to understand.

I have a sitter we had to hire ourselves. She is coming tomorrow with a three-year-old child. This is my only hope for getting someone here that we can afford. More later.

27 September 1994

I miss my quilt—Richard and Carol's quilt. It was with me during the worst time, and it helped me struggle to recover, and now it has left me feeling its loss, something I never anticipated. And, strangely, Cynthia called tonight, not long after Richard left. She probably is the only person I know who would understand about the way I feel about this quilt and finally giving it up. She told me she feels the same loss when she sends a finished manuscript off to be published.

Now I must work on my *Symphony* series. There is a lot of work ahead, but it is all figured out. All I have to do is follow my own instructions.

6 October 1994

This is the anniversary (if you could call it that) of my last hospitalization. A year ago I went through the worst ordeal of my life. I came through it and even finished the desert quilt and another quilt for Julie.

10 October 1994

Things are better. Hospice seems to be working out okay. I want to stay calm. I want to let go quietly. Then why did I scream (or try to scream) at Eddie and the supplier when they refused to acknowledge my presence while they were adjusting my oxygen flow? Eddie says, "That sounds right." The oxygen guy: "See, you put the frames in the perimeter and attach this valve." I say (too loudly), "Why

Pat working on niece Angie's quilt on her studio bed

don't you ask me how it feels or show me how to fix it, since I am the one using it?" Later we interviewed for a sitter once again.

15 October 1994

Sometimes I will begin having trouble while I am writing. I will just lose the thread somehow, all of a sudden. I owe four letters right now because I don't want to do this in a letter to one of my nieces.

19 October 1994

We now have a sitter whom we really want to keep, but I think we are going to lose her because of the pets. My breathing is terrible. Cynthia came by today, and I was so glad to see her. I got to tell her about my new project.

For the last two days, my Hospice team has been trying to get me to take medication to help reduce my anxiety. They stress the importance of staying calm when my breathing is very difficult. I say, "The anxiety drug interferes with my breathing and makes it very hard work." But today I got so upset I said, "I give up," and swallowed a pill. Well, thirty minutes later I felt my back relaxing. Now I see the point. There is not much they can do about the actual problem, but if I use the anxiety and pain medication, it won't be so difficult for me.

I know this is a final "letting go." I am not sure how it will go from here on. Tomorrow I plan to get all my notes together on my *Symphony* series and copy them down in here. I have it all worked out, except for the adjustments that have to be made to accommodate the inevitable surprises.

16 November 1994

The new pills have worked out so well. I am able to cough for longer periods without hunger for air. They have taken the fear away. I have decided to back away from the sitter idea for now. As long as I can manage, I want to. I hate to spend so much money on something that really is not at all helpful. Eddie was off three days this past weekend and he will be off all week Thanksgiving week. No problem pending.

To qualify for Hospice my doctor only had to say that in his opinion I had six months or less to live. I figure (*I always play with the numbers*) by April I will have my *Symphony* series done, the tops for certain. Nobody really knows how long I will last, of course, but it pushes me, and I need a push.

I haven't written much in my journals lately. I have felt so much better, I have done a lot of catching up writing letters.

This next week I wanted to have everyone for Thanksgiving, but Eddie put a damper on that. He asked if I was going to include the Hospice people who are working with me. OK, OK, OK. It was unrealistic, but I felt so good for the first time in so long. We'll order a ham and pies, but maybe I'll fix a cheesecake and, for sure, some dressing. More tomorrow.

21 November 1994

Countdown to Thanksgiving. Everyone's coming for dessert after eating out. And now one of my nieces, Angie, who is getting married in May, asked me tonight if she could get married here at our house! Well, I was surprised but said yes. The couple are in their early twenties, and I am a sucker. No, if they want to do this, and I'm alive (*this is meant as a joke*), we'll pull it off. I know everyone will help out. At first my mother was upset. Angie's mother, my sister Jodie, seemed okay with the idea. My other sister, Anne, too. She and I got to talking about family expectations and surprises, especially around the holidays. We had to laugh. As long as there are families, there will be these weird goings-on.

24 November 1994 (Thanksgiving)

2:00 a.m. I have just sat down here in my studio/hospital bed. I am probably the only artist with a studio that has bed rails. Today I have probably been on my feet more than I have been for months. I made dressing the old-fashioned way—it took hours—and I made a chocolate cheesecake. We bought a ham and all the fixings, and tonight we've just settled down. Eddie has been trying to clean while I cook. It has almost felt normal, except that I couldn't stand at the kitchen counter so I sat on my lovely commode chair, which we set on top of a case of Cokes so I would be high enough to work. I felt so good being able to do this, at least this one more time. How many *one more times* have I done this now? It has become quite a family joke.

29 November 1994

I do find myself repeating words more, and sometimes entire sentences. This bothers me no end and I seem to have no control over it. I have muscle spasms, as well, in my hands and arms and …

2 December 1994

I stopped the above because I was just complaining. I guess my problem is like the guy (Peter Sellers, I think) in the sixties movie "*Dr. Strangelove, or How I Learned to Stop Worrying and Love the Bomb.*" My hand or foot will just jerk unexpectedly. "What fresh hell is this?" (*grumbles Dorothy Parker*). But it is not such a big deal. It makes life more interesting in a way.

4 December 1994

I cannot remember when bathing in my bathtub became such a difficult operation, but it has—to the point where I now pray for strength to get through it. Today, as I stared at the tiles, I asked and then answered that old nagging question, just as we did in my catechism classes a hundred years ago: "*Q—Why did God make you? A—God made me to know, love, and serve Him in this world.*" One of my nieces joked recently that being a Catholic is sort of like being a part of the Mafia. You may think you have left, but you never can quit! How could I ever forget the Mass after walking to church every day with my grandmother when I was living with her after high school. It was during this time that my grandmother saved my life. Only now have I started to understand how complicated that life has been.

As I work on my *Symphony* series, my niece who has studied ballet keeps coming to mind. I have a whole folder of dancers in every position.

6 December 1994

Something really wonderful has happened. My sister Anne has sent me a little featherweight sewing machine for Christmas. I am overwhelmed. She's been so good to me and her children have added so much to my life. Now this. I had told Eddie some time ago that I wished I had a small machine that I could use in bed, so I could lie back on my pile of pillows when my back or chest got to hurting. I am such a dreamer, I had no idea that Eddie soon had Mother and Katie looking all over to hunt one down. When they couldn't find one, I guess they called Anne, and she mailed it to Mother. I feel like this big, spoiled baby. *"I need this, I want that."* I don't expect things like this, *but* I can't wait to begin using it.

31 December 1994

This is the end of 1994. As I glance back over this book, I realize my journal, which I intended to keep so neat and organized, has become a true reflection of the turmoil that exists on this hospital bed where I have to clear out a little space just to get my legs flat.

I have also had a great deal of mental confusion since Christmas. They say this is due to a lack of sufficient oxygen. I can't remember. I can't finish sentences or thoughts. One day this week I will try to write again. I repeat myself, I repeat myself, I repeat myself. (*Sometimes humor helps.*)

9 January 1995

Today I realized something I want to put words to, if this is possible. In almost all my relationships now, the cards and letters I receive and save seem more real to me than the people who send them. I can't say whether this is some kind of paranoia or a blinding flash of truth. But after several days of complete confusion last week, the truth, as I see it, is that I am already gone. To most friends and family, when I stop breathing (forever) it will be a formality. And yet I can still feel such passion for my quilts. I wonder why.

11 January 1995

I remember lying beside my maternal grandmother as a small child and feeling how soft her arm was. I marvel, as I grow older and see my own skin soften, at how close our ages, hers then and mine today, have become. Sometimes even, as now, when my mother sits here beside me, I dream of lying beside her mother and being held in her arms again.

18 January 1995

They are going to re-carpet the house (not one minute too soon) to have it fresh for Angie's wedding here. I would like to finish her little quilt, and now Jodie has asked me to do a banner for her wedding later this spring.

23 January 1995

I can see myself, like poor, crazed Van Gogh, experiencing my quilts in a room with no one but me, my dog, and the music. My mother, off in the kitchen, will say, "I knew she was doing too much." My husband will say, "When you get through there, honey, I need to ask you where the checks (or keys, or socks) are." My dog will think, "Isn't this wonderful, and it was all done for me."

FuFu

Later. I really need to write Cynthia and talk to her. I want her to know me better, but it has been hard to drag my past, which I have tried to put behind me, into the positive picture that she has had of me as a student and now as an artist. Tomorrow I will call her and write as well.

29 January 1995

Dear Cynthia,

It seems to me now that I spend lots of wasted time searching for things in this square footage that is my "studio," as sometimes I wonder what truth it is that's buried somewhere in what serves as my memory. Lately I have been better, and so my thinking is better, meaning that I don't feel my mind, because of my body, is about to shatter and fall into a thousand pieces.

I have been doing remarkably well recently. I mention this only because the people who fill out the myriad forms connected to my health conundrum say I have moved from "terminal critical" to "terminal stable," and this affects who pays what to whom. Needless to say, we're caught off guard by the fact that I have been given another reprieve, or maybe my freedom has been delayed. All of this aside, the simple truth is, I have been feeling better and have started working on two more "ideas." One of my sisters asked if I could make a wedding banner for her, and this is one that has evolved into something I want to do even if it does not work out to be suitable for the occasion. The other project is one begun earlier with strips sewn together, then rearranged into something else. My new, small machine has made everything so much simpler to work out. I then appliqué over it.

At last, also, I am well enough to write some and to have some new carpet put in before my niece's wedding. She and he are getting married March 18th at 1:30 p.m. I hope, if you have the time, you will come. They had trouble getting a priest in Memphis to marry them in a private home. One of the liberal priests in Mississippi is coming to marry them, so everything is all set.

It seemed like time to check in with you ...

Love,

Pat

11 March 1995

My lifetime Hospice benefit has run out, but I have not. So where to go from here? Medicare won't cover. Appeal? I am so tired of all the paperwork involved now. How does one know when the situation changes from *critical* to *stable chronic*? Anyway, I am here, and quite honestly feeling better. The fear that I won't be able to keep up the struggle to breathe has gone for the moment. The worst part of this sickness is fear. I have to work on it all the time.

26 March 1995

Tonight I got out a couple of my old art history books to read, and some *Art in America* magazines. I always feel excited when I do this. It makes me feel that I am part of a continuum, an unbroken line of artists. It helps me to remember why I struggled through school, how I wanted to learn all I could about art and artists, and how I wanted to leave something of myself for the next generation.

28 March 1995

I decided *not* to have the transplant. It was too drastic, too extreme, and I was afraid I would not have the stamina to get through it. This is as honest as I can be. I tried to say, and tell myself, that I felt someone younger should have the new lungs, but the real reason for deciding not to complete the preliminary tests and get on a waiting list was pure fear—the fear that I could not make it through such a radical surgery, or that I might well survive and find myself in a world of endless pain. Maybe it was a lack of faith, but it really got my attention when I found out that I would have to have a bronchoscopic exam once a week. Such hell I am simply not willing to endure.

30 March 1995

I finished my yellow journal tonight, but I am not finished yet and I have more to say. Angie's wedding here in our living room has now become part of the family's history. It was beautiful, and the two of them seemed to be very much in love. Angie herself has such a sweet and beautiful personality, and I love them all for having the wedding here where I could be present. I've missed their events for the last few years: the weddings, graduations from college and high school. This wedding was another *gift*, a chance to experience once more the ties that join us, one to another, as a family.

31 March 1995

Last week I asked my niece Natalie if she would like to learn to paint silk with me this summer. I feel well enough to do it, I think. At any rate, she seems interested. I gave her my new book on silk painting, something I have been wanting to try. I am supposed to create a banner for Jodie and Monty's wedding. I have only until May 20th, so I won't have time for a quilt. Mother, who's agreed to help get it done, suggests using glue and black strips for outlines like those in my stained glass design. No sewing. Okay.

> [By April, I had decided to put together a book based on Pat's art and life and asked her to see what she had in the way of materials. Her reply, in a letter of April 18, revealed for the first time how much she had written, far surpassing anything I had expected. "Here I have journals all over the place," she said, "but they attest to my scattered mind and life, and only since 1990. I tried to keep my sickness journal separate from my working notes, and my spiritual journal separate from my family journal. Well, how long do you think it took me to realize that they are all one person's life," one story of a woman trying "to cope and leave behind something besides her long struggle with chronic illness?"]

2 May 1995

My mother told me the other day that my flowers outside, the roses and peonies, are full of blooms. We have let them go for so long, I couldn't believe it. I hate to add anything to Eddie's duties, and he is not much interested in flowers, but I wish there was someone who would care for them. I have never been able to smell them, but I have always loved the *feel* of a rose. When I used to cut one from the bush and hold it against my cheek, its cool softness and perfect beauty, like a baby's cheek against mine, brought a rush of exquisite joy I cannot express

This morning Cynthia called and proposed a plan to do some sort of book about my work.

8 May 1995

I have finished Jodie's wedding banner. I think it may not be as simple as she wanted it, and I was unsure of how she would react. But once I began mixing colors for it, I just kept on going and ended up with fabrics in all shades and hues of red: some were metallic lamés, some marbleized red tones, and some hand-dyed pieces of red-orange and red-purple. Then I put the two azaleas on a backdrop of sky-to-earth blues, blue-greens, and teal. I took some Polaroids and went back and adjusted some of the color. Today I finished by putting some tabs across the top to hang it. Jodie said she is going to try and take it to the reception.

I used to be neat, blonde, always on time—whatever happened to my life? I am messy, gray, and there is no time to be on. Time has very little meaning.

Eddie and I both watched *Shadowlands* last night, and I was so surprised that he liked the movie. Usually he doesn't like tearjerkers, but I think he appreciated this one for its honesty in dealing with death and the love that ends or goes on in pain. It also raised the question of whether God wants us to suffer. I think Anthony Hopkins, who played C.S. Lewis, said at one point, "We are blocks of stone and are chiseled out by a God who wants us to grow to be creatures who can love and be loved."

Jodie's wedding banner

13 May 1995

Yesterday the children next door left a poem, or really three poems they wrote on the family's computer, in our front door. I enjoy these little reminders that life goes on in the world outside.

Next weekend we will be having Wedding Number 2 in our living room, with all the relatives and all the emotions. Cynthia's minister friend, Cheryl Cornish, is going to marry Jodie and Monty.

14 May 1995, My 52nd Birthday

Tonight all the correspondence I keep in this journal nearly fell out. I have kept it all here with my writing because it is so much a part of my story and my secret of survival. I want to leave these letters and cards so the next generation can see what a rich life a person can have even when she can no longer live outside four walls. Or maybe to show how having kind people and fulfilling work like my quilting can keep one's life going in a way that seems meaningful. If these journals contained only my words and concern with myself and had no evidence of the people who have taken time to be with me—sharing their wit and hopes and successes—then you would only have part of the story. These people are tucked in here, and I am going to make another fabric pouch to hold their letters and cards, like the pouch with my yellow journal, which is now full.

20 May 1995

It was a wonderful day. Jodie and Monty's wedding went well. Cynthia and Cheryl came, which also meant much to me, and they stayed to visit after the others went on to the reception.

We talked about dropping the masks we wear to let others see that we need them and love them. I told them about how my sickness has brought me to where I can do this. I used to be distant and sharp to cover a lot of my anger and pain. Now I can finally try to make things right with the people who matter to me.

[One afternoon, a large, rotten oak that stood next to the house crashed to the ground. Miraculously, its descent just missed on one side the den where the Clines had been sitting and on the other the neighbors' pool, which was packed with children. "Another reprieve," Pat said to me, when recounting this latest brush with death.]

24 May 1995

Yesterday I felt so optimistic as I got out my Victorian quilt and saw that I had gotten farther along on it than I remembered. It had been too long on the shelf, covered with tissue paper, and it will be a joy to finish it here in bed, where my back is supported. I have the stained-glass block in my lap now and am amazed at how much stitching went into the little circular piece in the corner. I have stacks of notes on what I intended to do. I see also that this was all done before my last illness in the hospital, at a point when I was more together in many ways. I am so glad I got it all figured out then and wrote it all down, and purchased everything I needed. I can do what I have to do now without any physical or mental involvement. Anne's getting this little sewing machine for me has made this last stage possible. I can do this in no time, I know, and tomorrow's another day.

26 May 1995

Early in our relationship, Eddie was spending a lot of time with my mother's mother, who was very ill. She was the person I felt closest to, and when she died in her early eighties, I was devastated. Somehow, in the years since then, Eddie has taken my grandmother's place. It sounds very strange, even to me, but Eddie himself says this is true.

2 June 1995

Today, after Cynthia's call, I understand better the kind of project she has in mind and why she thinks people who are total strangers would benefit. The words from the movie *Shadowlands* come to mind: *"We read to know we are not alone."*

29 June 1995

At this time I have in progress four *Symphony* quilts, back and front; one large Victorian crazy quilt; a hexagon quilt; a bargello quilt; and this *Memphis Blues*. There are twelve altogether, counting the fronts and backs of the *Symphony*.

6 July 1995

I have a pair of silver, spiked, high heels I have kept from the sixties to prove that I once was insane, but am okay now. I seldom wear shoes at all anymore.

Today I got a postcard from Jean, the Eucharistic minister. The volunteer work she does, visiting and bringing us old and sick people Communion, is something new for me, and she has turned out to be another wonderful person in my life.

[As work on the book got under way, Pat caught my enthusiasm and started providing basic information. A letter in early July was typical.]

13 July 1995
Cynthia,

I may be overloading you, but … to know me involves knowing who I love and whose love I feel and have felt. So I'll put a little family tree (or trees) below, so you can see who belongs to whom.

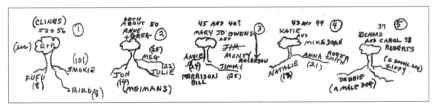

I will not have a quiz on this. Our mother is Mary Margaret Roberts. Our father, Richard Roberts, died in 1965.

Pat

16 July 1995

Last night I listened to Eddie talk about the navy. He says sometimes he misses it still. I remember how, when I was younger, I would answer by saying, *"War is wrong,"* until he hardly ever mentioned the years he spent in the service. I would try to explain the idea of world peace, which seemed simple enough to me. But I have come to realize that the time in the navy *he* misses is really the time of his youth—when the starlit nights and the open sea seemed to promise a future of infinite possibilities. I wasn't listening closely, but I let him tell me about it all—the ships and the guns and the clouds and the sky—and I realized that these were the years he grew up. It was only later, when he went to Vietnam, that he became disillusioned. Both of us learned the hard way how to get past broken dreams, physical pain, and permanent loss. Maybe this is why we made it together. Our twentieth anniversary is this month.

24 July 1995

Tonight on the news was a very well-done profile on Rosa Parks. I've known about her for years and years, but we had no TV in 1955, and so here I *saw* for the first time how courageous she actually was. I saw how important her seemingly small act of defiance was for her race and for *all* Americans. I've heard so many white people say they are not responsible for slavery, for something that went on before they were born. But I think I am responsible for my failure to see the old plantation attitudes that were carried over into my lifetime. My black neighbors were being treated like second-class citizens and in many cases, still are, but I never paid close attention. I never acknowledged it. So this is one more thing I must do before I go.

29 July 1995

At last I have made some headway on my *Symphony* (*"Overture"*). Only one major mistake: I sewed one whole strip to the wrong side of another strip. I could not believe I did this! Such a waste. I am going to have to double-check each step as I proceed from the center outward. It is so easy to get confused with these triangles in seven gradations of color, and the colors are all intense, too. (*Here, a clash of cymbals!*) But I have taken all the wrong stitches out—machine stitches—removed very carefully because the fabrics are very fragile. Now, I am back in the flow of things.

2 August 1995

I received another letter from my doctor. He has mentioned my quilts as quilts before, when I took them to the Mid-South Fair and one year won a first-place ribbon with my Cathedral Window (*a little bragging here*). I got nothing for my *Enlightenment* at the fair, but Natalie took a photo of it hanging up with all the traditional others and it did *sing*; you *had* to look at it, even if you didn't like it. When I sent my doctor the photo of the desert quilt, he wrote back enthusiastically, and even more enthusiastically when I told him about the new quilts. Yet he called these projects good *therapy*, which is probably so, but they are so much more than that to me.

The above sounds like Judy Chicago wanting acceptance from the male culture. I may be asking too much. It is true that my quilts were made because I was sick and confined, and they gave me a way to reach out to my family and friends. But now I am making quilts—my *Victorian Echo* and my *Symphony*—for myself and all of my soul sisters, whose spirits are present in every shade and every hue of these soft, strong fabrics. They are my gift and my progeny, and they are *art!*

10 August 1995

Yesterday Cynthia spent some time here, and each time she visits, I am amazed at how much she knows about me that I don't know she knows. It is unsettling. I cannot imagine having written so freely in the journals I gave her, unless it was in an old journal I kept for her class when I was in college. I had recently had a mastectomy and felt I was having a breakdown of some sort. We cannot find that first journal, but Cynthia still had all the details in place. I was so relieved. I've worried these last few weeks and months, ever since she told me she wanted to do a book, about being less than truthful with her. I remember somewhere someone saying, "I have told a lie for so long, I cannot remember what the truth is." I have never forgotten how wild and destructive I was in my early years, or that I still have many shortcomings, but I had not remembered writing about them and was afraid to tell her—afraid of losing someone I deeply respect. I am not sure how our friendship evolved. The beginning of relationships is as hard to pinpoint as the beginning of a life. Did this one begin about ten years ago, or this week when the truth of my life was recited back to me gently, carefully, unmistakably—while the two of us were sewing?

Cynthia was enlarging the neck of a T-shirt by removing the inside strip piece and turning under the ribbing. Why did I write this here? I guess it's like the time I was being released from the rehab unit and had to take oxygen home with me for the first time. The head nurse came in for a last-minute check, an "Everything okay?" kind of thing. I was trying to open a pill bottle and she was watching me. She could probably tell I was also struggling not to cry about needing the oxygen, and she took the pills out of my hands and said, "I'm going to give you some *good* news." She took a key and pressed it into a groove and out popped the childproof ring that gives me fits opening pill bottles. "You will never have to struggle with a 'pop cap' again," she said. It was simple and obvious, but I would never have thought of it myself. The bigger problems I have to work out on my own, but thanks to the women who have taught me their tricks, I won't have to wrestle with any more safety caps or wear my T-shirts with necklines that fit too close.

30 August 1995

Here I must confess the *Overture* piece is driving me crazy (or *crazier*). Mother came over while I was unsewing a row of the gradations that had gotten out of line and thrown off the whole design. She had said she would help me out by cutting fabric, but, instead, she suggested an easier way for cutting out the tiny squares from the fabric ahead of time and keeping the different shades separate by storing them in plastic sandwich bags. This will keep them from getting mixed up. I may try this. She also said that she had better not cut any fabric for me because it would probably not be right. Then Mother told me about a woman who goes to church with her and Katie, and lately has been coming with a little oxygen tank slung over her shoulder as if nothing were wrong. The bulletin Sunday asked for prayers because she is having a heart/lung transplant. I try *not* to react to heroic stories that make me look bad by doing something completely stupid. I know Mother probably did not intend to be putting me down. I just get defensive easily when I feel that people think I could do more physically, if I only tried to get out and around. "Well, let me know how this surgery goes," I say. "Well, I've gotta go," she says.

3 September 1995

This week I plan to do some of the silk painting on the backing of the four pieces in the *Symphony* series. When this is accomplished, the series will actually be composed of eight compositions.

13 September 1995

Sometimes I feel like I work so hard and there is so little to show for it. I hate whining, therefore I whine.

23 September 1995

Today I talked to Cynthia a long time. It feels so strange to realize how much of my life, or myself, I have given over to her. In an odd way she may be able to deal with all my skeletons in the closets and the elephant in the living room better than I.

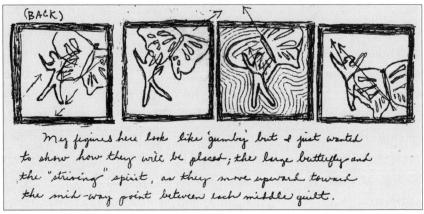

(BACK)

My figures here look like 'gumby' but I just wanted to show how they will be placed; the large butterfly and the "striving" spirit, as they move upward toward the mid-way point between each middle quilt.

Sketches of large butterfly and "striving spirit" on backs of Symphony *series*

25 September 1995

Tonight on late-night radio a doctor said he thought kindness "is the best medicine." I know this has been true for me. People's kindness to me has helped me calm down and rebound. And looking at it from the other end, if the people on whom I rely are irritable, if I am kind, they usually don't stay upset. This seems to fly in the face of all I know about self-esteem and not letting people push you around by being too nice, but for me, a captive of a disease that has made me dependent on medicines, doctors, nurses, therapists, and family members all my life, kindness works when all else fails.

26 September 1995

My old dog, the gray poodle Smokey, started howling today, and I knew he was dying, as my other dog did a while back. He had only been with us for five or six years, but he truly was part of the family. He had belonged to a man who had recently died of cancer when Smokey and I first met. I was working on a fund-raising benefit for the Crisis Center with the man's widow. She was an older woman who was planning to sell her house and she mentioned putting Smokey to sleep. He was too much trouble, she said. He just seemed to want attention—and even though she said he was thirteen years old, he was healthy enough. Eddie and I went and picked him up, and he took to Eddie from the first. Until the past few weeks he was fine. He slept all the time, but yesterday and today he was no longer fine. So instead of letting him die like our other dog, Pee Dee, groaning and seeming to be in pain, Eddie held him while he died quickly at the vet's office. I felt so sorry for Eddie when he came home. What a life he has with all of us!

1 October 1995

Yesterday Cynthia came over and brought back the squares of fabric that she and Cheryl had cut out for me. She asked me if I was keeping this journal any differently now that I know other people will someday be reading what I write. As I think about this, my answer would have to be "yes and no."

If we write, as we read, to know we are not alone—and I believe we do—then all of us write in journals feeling at some level that someone might read what we put on the pages, especially if we have something we want to set straight. The artist in me wants to be understood, wants to explain herself. This must be one of the reasons I write as much as I can about my ideas and try to work out my designs and what makes me respond to something as I do. The illness I have wants to be understood, too. It's like living in a coastal town during bad weather. At one moment there is a damaging wind, at the next, a hurricane or tornado. So, much of my life now is putting things back together and explaining through my journals and my quilts. After all my verbose agonizing about my private self being exposed, I've decided that all that matters in the end is honorable intentions all around and remaining trustworthy, truthful, and kind.

8 October 1995

Last night I finished trying to write about my father for my brother, who hardly knew him. Maybe it will forever be one of those unfinished melodies. I know that at least I tried to go back, and I have (rather dramatically) sewn in my efforts, actually stitching the pieces of paper into this book with black thread so I can come back here and find them if ever I want to try again. In a novel, *Family Pictures*, the narrator starts to understand herself and her family when she sees that all of her memories have their place and value. Even the bad ones were necessary because they were part of the family album. She did not have to make sense of them all and she certainly could not change them. She could only take what she was given and go from there.

10 October 1995

Mother came over to visit and caught me with my little plastic bags as I was trying to organize the colored squares for the *Symphony* quilt. She said the NOW vigil and protesters have been hounding O.J. Simpson since he was found not guilty of killing his wife and her friend. This restored at least some of my faith in the way women have been reacting to last week's verdict. What has really upset me the most is the way the domestic abuse issue has been ignored or lost amid all the discussion of race.

13 October 1995

I remember a couple of teachers in college telling me something I had done was idealistic. When I asked if this was good or bad, one of them only said it was unusual, and the other didn't say anything— he just walked off. I always wondered what they meant.

19 October 1995

The worst has happened. I am having some sort of problem with my right hand. Since I have been awake, about two hours now, I have lost the strength in it, as if it has gone to sleep, and the feeling has not come back in my right smallest finger and the finger next to it. I cannot make a fist. *But* more importantly, it seems to be getting worse. I stopped and tried to lift my water. *Okay*. To straighten the room up. *Ditto*. I don't have trouble with larger things, but with writing, yes; and I cannot paint the designs on my *Symphony*'s silk backings. I wanted to do that first thing, while I was still rested up and had my daily grace period before I started coughing again. I called my doctor and Eddie to report this. Eddie said he has had the same thing happen to him. He always says this. He told me about how he almost cut two of his fingers off once, and how long they were numb. I couldn't remember this accident, and suddenly I was so overwhelmed with sympathy and affection for Eddie that made me realize how much I have focused on myself and not paid attention to him. Tonight I will do something special for him. Maybe bake cookies? (Maybe part of my *brain* has been numbed?) My doctor said it may just be a pinched nerve. Call him tomorrow if it is still the same. Actually, my writing is already better. It was just a relief to hear "a pinched nerve." It may just take a while to get back to normal.

20 October 1995

My hand is a little better, fear quieted. I can manage, I think, if it gets no worse, but I hope it will clear up because it still makes me clumsy. I can't hold the weight of something. FuFu is tired of having me dropping things on him. Can an artist manage painting on silk in bed? This is truly the biggest challenge I have had so far.

22 October 1995

Disregard all previous notes on silk painting. It is now 2 a.m. and so far I have been very, very fortunate, as I never imagined I would. I finally spread the four backings for my *Symphony* out on wet plastic here in the den, behind the chair, while FuFu was on the other side, safely out of trouble. I worked steadily for hours—I lost track of time—as I mixed my dye and pretreated the silk, fixed the designs, and lay them out to dry, all this in my humble abode, with FuFu just inches away from ruining everything.

26 October 1995

So much is going on. My silk pieces, after all, have been so *satisfying*. I cannot think of a way to express the pleasure this dyeing and washing and ironing process has given me. Today I work on the butterflies, the large one first. Tonight I will photograph what I have done.

3:30 p.m. I'm still working. Nothing new on that front. But, for some odd reason, I have been thinking about my death certificate, which is in a folder with my Hospice stuff. I think that I must be very unusual in that this document is already signed (with the date to be added at the appropriate time).

I remember my doctor saying on my medical record that he did not believe I would ever be able to cope outside of a hospital, and now, here I am, two years later, *coping* all over the place. I should not be flip about my life, my quilts, my latest triumph with silk, but why be serious when I feel so wonderful? I can imagine that a professional might say that it is the manic phase of manic-depressive symptoms. *But who cares?* Thank goodness for this reprieve.

31 October 1995

In some amazing way, I am still feeling unbelievably well and have gotten much done, though anyone looking on might not see this.

Later. Late night. Everything suddenly went wrong today. Actually one thing went wrong today and colored everything else. My little dog, whom I love more than most people seem to understand, had a long seizure this afternoon, and I thought I had lost him a couple of times. His seizure lasted ten or fifteen minutes, and twice he stopped breathing. I tried reviving him mouth to mouth, and he responded by taking a quick breath and moving slightly. It was the worst thing physically and emotionally that I've been through. I called my sister Jodie and asked if she could help. I was afraid that the longer the seizure lasted, the worse the effects might be. She came over and took him to Dr. Kelley's, and he has some medicine now. Then I felt so bad about troubling Jodie, but I knew that she is also an animal person. Right now, I can't write any more.

14 November 1995

I still cannot write or think straight. I am smothered, overcome by FuFu's death. Why is this? I remind myself that children die every day from illnesses or, worse, from abuse and neglect, from starvation and war. Yet this is no help. A dear little bully of a dog is gone forever. I will never hold him again, and my heart has gone, too.

15 November 1995

I'm taking a minute to write and rest my back from hand-sewing butterflies. I have had a little distraction and now have quit crying. Julie brought Italian food for supper. Mother and Katie and Jodie have called. I know they all realize how much I loved FuFu. I am thinking about us getting another dog, both for Eddie's sake and so I will not have such an empty room. It is hard to wake up and have no one to talk to. Even the bird has been acting strange. He doesn't bark anymore, for one thing. I wonder if he doesn't miss the dogs, too. A year ago I had two, and now there are none. Anyway I gave my sinuses a chance to clear up from all the tears, at least until the mail came with an article Cynthia sent us about the wall, the Vietnam War Memorial. We had planned to go there someday, and I believe Eddie will still go at some point.

When I was in college, I did a drawing project on Vietnam, which I still have somewhere. It's mixed media, I think: a map and a helicopter and fire. It was very odd—the class, that is. The assignment was to do something we were trying to come to terms with, and I can distinctly remember what two of the others turned in. One was by a young girl who did a pencil rubbing of the headstone on her mother's grave and added a cigarette package and maybe a photo of herself as a child with her mother. That one has never left me. The other I remember was a bright self-portrait in neonlike pastels by a young man who said he was sometimes suicidal. His drawing was so expressive and well executed that I had a feeling we might be seeing a real artist there in the making. However, he missed class constantly and fell asleep once. I was careful not to say I was really impressed with his work because I suspected that he was not getting along with the adult world, but I felt bad seeing how lost he was. I have wondered whatever became of him.

17 November 1995

Our old home in Houston, Mississippi, is now a bed-and-breakfast inn. This is really a fact, but is also a joke for all of us except Mother. My brother, Richard, and his wife, Carol, stayed there recently when they went to his class reunion. Richard stayed in his old room upstairs and said he felt he was in the twilight zone. Mother left nearly all of the furnishings there, and the new owners had only changed a few things. As Thanksgiving approaches, we have been swapping anecdotes like these, and there will be others. This is why I hate not being there at Katie's this year.

Last week I ordered my Uncle Pat a book, *Domers: A Year at Notre Dame*. I called him to tell him he has a gift coming. He has always taken very seriously his role as my godfather, and he has stood by me, even during my wildest days. I've always felt that in his orderly world I may have been his only failure, and this is why I have tried for the past few years to show him how much I appreciate him. He was in the emergency room when I landed there during my terrible twenties, and he came to the airport to see us off when we flew to the Mayo Clinic many years later. As we started to board the plane, I turned and went back to hug him. It was the first time I had ever hugged him, and yet he had always stood by me.

29 November 1995

And here's our little Fu II (Fu Two), our new puppy pug. He has "kennel cough," the dog doctor says. So he coughs, and then I cough. I've worked out an exercise plan for him now. I put him in the kitchen while I sit at the door, on this side of the gate in a chair. Bless his little heart. He runs and runs, then he wants to play, which I do as best I can. I am having a problem with him biting. The more excited he gets, the more out of control. Then when I can't manage any longer, he goes back to his bed in the box and falls asleep. I would give anything to be stronger right now because I want him to be better trained than FuFu. I hate to have people who know me thinking that having this "baby" was a bad idea. Eddie wanted to fix things,

Fu Two

and we really do care for this little guy. He goes wild when he hears Eddie's voice. Eddie plays with Fu Two better than I do. He gets down on the floor and, watching the two of them, I am grateful he got the little dog. When FuFu died, he said, "I don't know what I would do if something happened to you. I wouldn't have anyone to come home to." I do not mind that the dog and I share this importance in his life.

1 December 1995

Yesterday when I could not walk for an hour and did not improve much as the day wore on, I called my home care people to see if antibiotics might help, though I'm not even sure about them anymore. A nurse came out and filled out pages of stuff. She asked about the living will, and I asked about whether my organs (liver, kidneys, etc.) could be used by someone else, given my disease and given genetics. (I have wondered about this, but never asked.) She said that probably only my corneas would be transplantable. Other organs will be destroyed as my lungs go. Well, never ask a question you don't want to hear the answer to.

I am going to stop here. I have had trouble talking today; I keep saying things backwards, and I don't know where it comes from. I am not taking more medicine, or I might think it was coming from there. I just cannot think straight. I got out my things to sew, then I was too uncoordinated.

I cannot get beyond sitting and staring (the worst outcome for anybody). It is as if I am on an elevator going down. It stops at difficult levels, and I can get out for a while, but then I have to return for the next descent.

> [I myself had started keeping a set of diaries in 1991, during a convalescence from mononucleosis. Initially I had felt a need to give my long days some substance and shape by capturing whatever minutia distinguished the one from the next. Then my entries became more varied and animated as I regained my mobility. My casual references to them piqued Pat's curiosity, and eventually she asked if she might read them.]

5 December 1995

I stopped everything else and read Cynthia's journal from front to back. Reading a little and putting it aside was not giving me a clear picture, but reading straight through, I saw her move through her days with determination, even when her own body was not working as well as it might. I was surprised at some of the things she sees going on in high places and I want to talk to her about how women like us can deal with such things. Sharing her journal has added another dimension to our relationship. *"I went to Kroger's, drove to school, came back, and sat in a cozy chair"*—it was almost as if I *lived* in the outside world again. I *saw* the carved pumpkins out around Halloween and *saw* the falling leaves. (To add insult to injury, my two trees, an oak and a sweet gum, fell over this year. They weren't in any better shape than I am.) What I mean is, I was reminded of how I used to think and feel as I read about the days to which she gave color and shape.

Home health care is going to try to put me on new IV antibiotics tomorrow. The male nurse came out today to get a "line" in but will have to come back tomorrow. I am *not* going back to the hospital to have a catheter put in. That would be the next step, but if it comes to that I will just forgo the antibiotics. I feel this nurse will get it set up in the morning. One of my neighbors stopped him and asked him who he was. I guess he had never seen a nurse making rounds on a motorcycle before.

12 December 1995

A woman who works in my doctor's office called me today to tell me how much she enjoyed the draft of the article Cynthia wrote about me for the University of Memphis alumni magazine, which mentioned my work with the Crisis Center. This touched her, she said, because her husband committed suicide four years ago, and she has had such a hard time, especially at the holidays, coming to terms with it. I told her she will be on my mind and in my heart and prayers. She is always so pleasant, this soft-spoken blonde with a southern accent, always doing two or three things at once, yet going from one person to the next without seeming rushed. She is me if I had stayed with my "medical secretarial" courses and the first job I had in Memphis in 1963. Only I wore high heels and expensive outfits at first, before the long hours converted me to wearing a white uniform and flat shoes. This morning, as Eddie struggled to help me in the bathroom before he left for work, I admitted to him I could not pray anymore. It was 6 a.m. and I was exhausted and realized this was true. But then I told my doctor's receptionist I would pray for her, and I did. I prayed for us both today, though I still just don't know about prayer.

Cynthia and Pat, June 1996

14 December 1995

Because I have been so sick recently, both Eddie and I have been miserable. I've written him a letter tonight to try to get back to a better state and lift his burden after these awful days. I told him how much I valued his love and appreciated that he has stood by me, when he could have left long ago.

I have to say here, as I look back over these jottings, that I have been able to straighten out my feet. The toenails on both feet were in very bad shape and got worse with each new bout of illness. I do not know why. But I have been blessed with well feet through medication and not wearing shoes for four years. Now my feet are lovely, but the rest of me is shot.

23 December 1995

Eddie has gone Christmas shopping. He likes to be surprised and always says he loves his gift, or gifts, no matter what I get him. I hate surprises, and many times over the years I have been upset by his presents, often without even knowing why. He has given me nice-enough gifts: once a folding umbrella, and another time a huge microwave oven that would not have fit on the counter had I been able to pick it up to put it there. The electric can opener was my early warning of what was to come. That year, my friend Linda, who died not long ago, got the same thing because our husbands had gone shopping together. A double insult! You would think by now, twenty years later, we would have cut this out, but *no*. I have kept and wear a watch that needs sizing so badly it almost goes up to my elbow. I have a heart bracelet that fits the same way, and I wear it just as proudly.

Meanwhile, we got the most beautiful Christmas card from a cousin of mine today, with this message:

> *Every time a hand reaches out to help another ...*
> *Every time someone puts anger aside and strives for*
>   *understanding ...*
> *Every time people forget their differences and realize their*
>   *love for each other ... that is Christmas.*

I think, no matter what, I will appreciate my gifts from Eddie this year.

Note: After this last sentence, I stopped to eat. Eddie brought home some Krystals with fries and chili. Thank goodness for the new drugs for indigestion. It is almost midnight. We are just beginning the evening. What is wrong with this picture?

I thought I might try to present a single day from start to finish so anyone who might read my journal forty years from now would be able to reexperience one small segment of my life. But I cannot seem to do it. Maybe it is because I am always in one place. The same place. My day changes only with interactions with other people who pass through or phone or send letters. Otherwise, I spend it alone in my bed in the den in the center of the house. Not totally alone of course. There is a bird here, and in the kitchen, until he gets over eating and tearing up everything in sight, a little dog, "Baby Fu" as we so unimaginatively call him. It is too dangerous now to let him run loose because of the oxygen and electrical cords, so we cannot be as close as my old Fu and I were.

It was comforting to read in Cynthia's journal that someone had lost a dog and felt the pain that I feel when I think about FuFu. I can still feel him in my arms sometimes, or right by my side as he used to be when I tried to clean up the birdseed and crawled around the floor with a hand-vac. His leaning against me always made vacuuming more difficult, but I loved him being there. For a while, after the last hospitalization, I was afraid I would die while we were together during the day, and I couldn't imagine what he would do, he was so high-strung. But the opposite happened, and I still feel, somehow, I should have been able to save him. I wish I could get over this. Tomorrow is Christmas Eve.

25 December 1995

11:45 p.m. We had a good Christmas. Some of the family came over late in the afternoon, and we all swapped gifts. We all say we are going to quit buying gifts, but I doubt that we will. Mother crocheted me a bunny doll in a housecoat and slippers and its hair in curlers. It is really cute. But are we not 53 and 74? She also bought me an angel at the craft fair. It is made from an antique quilt that had been cut up because it had frayed or mildew had ruined it, and it is cute, too. Too much candy. Too much food. My sister Katie got me some see-through boxes to help me protect all this fabric lying about. Eddie bought me a small storage table to keep on the right side of the bed. Spillover had gotten out of hand. He worked all day setting it up. He missed a ball game to do it, and he missed his afternoon nap, which he *never* misses. So, it was a nice day. No upsets.

29 December 1995

It's almost another year. Time for resolutions. I am not sure whether I have made any resolutions in the past, but I have begun to have a sense of drifting and I need a clearer focus and sense of direction. This happened to me in the hospital this last, fateful time. I felt I was on a sinking ship and had to push myself hard to get off and into a lifeboat mid-ocean. By setting my sights on that goal, I was able to start in again with new vigor, and I got things accomplished when I got back home. But now there is no escape but the ocean. Antibiotics no longer help much, and I can only call on my inner resources to work up to my potential in my present situation. And so I resolve that (1) I will organize my fabrics in the bins Katie gave me for Christmas, (2) I will make a ledger out of my new journal that Jodie gave me, and (3) I will manage to get the card table in here and try to expand work space in the den. I am trying to use space and time to better advantage.

31 December 1995

Sometimes I feel ashamed for having developed so little theologically. It didn't exactly fit in with my lifestyle when I was young, but in my thirties and forties and fifties, I really have had no excuse. For a long time, I simply did not want to rock the boat by looking at orthodox ideas too closely, and now there is really no time to study religion, and maybe no reason to. I think that I will slowly and quietly put up the books and just hope the Holy Spirit is with me in some measure anyway.

This is my last notation for 1995. Only five more years left to this century. Tonight the TV is on and we are in Times Square, New York, waiting for the ball to drop. I used to have to go out on New Year's Eve and be part of a big celebration somewhere. I liked being in a large crowd. Now, I *love* the small group I have—Eddie, Bird, Fu, and Fluffy, our very shy cat.

12:01, 1996. Eddie walked over here just now and kissed me.

1 January 1996

I have ordered a loud "no-fail" alarm clock. My clock does not wake me up any more. I am hoping my new plan to get on a regular work schedule will help me make better use of my time. I do *so* want to finish my work.

6 January 1996

One day about five years ago, when an old high school friend of mine visited, she asked, "What ever happened to your painting of the church?" She said it had looked so real on the canvas, she wondered if I had counted every brick. I myself had not thought of it since the summer our priest, hoping to keep me out of more teenage trouble, commissioned me to undertake this project, as Michelangelo had been engaged. This was one of those things someone else brings to you from their memory as a gift.

8 January 1996

I started out Sunday by putting the wrong medication in my eye: Lotrimin (an antifungal for my nails) instead of Visine. What a stupid thing to do, and I call myself overly cautious about my use of medicine! It felt like acid, and fortunately I had a big, full glass of water and just began flushing the eye. Eddie helped by getting a basin, and I called the poison control center and found flushing with water is the thing to do, and I felt okay. Eddie kept saying, "Bless your heart, things just keep happening to you," which made me want to scream (though I don't know why). I suddenly knew that things could be worse when I remembered my grandfather, who lost his eyesight right after I was born. I thought about him whenever my eye hurt. Now my eye is okay. Experience is a hard teacher.

13 January 1996

Last night Elizabeth Marshburn brought me several copies of the alumni magazine with the article about my quilts. The ram on Richard's quilt is even on the cover, and I am so proud. This exposure of my work is something way beyond anything I ever hoped for or dreamed of. Eddie took a copy to work and said he wants to give copies to certain people who came to my show at the bookstore. Mother

came over and got one. Now I must send one to my doctor and my sister Anne and my brother. Okay, it's time to get back to work. I had better put a lid on the excitement for a while.

26 January 1996

I always hated viewing art that the artist said doesn't mean anything. I could never make such a statement. These reverse sides of my *Symphony* pieces do have a meaning, and I have even found some lines of prose that could be their caption:

> *You shall be free indeed*
> *when your days are not*
> *without a care nor your nights*
> *without a want and a grief,*
> *but rather when these things*
> *girdle your life and*
> *yet you rise above them*
> *naked and unbound.*
> —Kahlil Gibran

Very recently, on a particularly bad day, I read through some old family prayer books and tried to imagine a spiritual figure holding me in its arms the way I held my niece just a few nights ago to comfort her. This seemed to relax my aching back and ease my struggle to breathe.

31 January 1996

The weather is very cold, in the teens the last couple of days. Our new furnace is not working, and the streets are so bad we can't get anyone out to fix it. So I'm working in a little ball here with my new vest on and an electric blanket thrown over me.

2 February 1996

The man who owns the heating and cooling business finally came to the house around noon to fix the system. At one point I heard a loud pop and saw sparks fly everywhere. I was afraid he'd been electrocuted. I wondered if CPR would be of any use to him if I tried it, and just as I was getting up, he stuck his head around the corner and asked where the circuit breaker was. After that I fell asleep, and when I woke up he was gone and it was warm. So much for my life as an artist in a den. I wonder what the man thought when he saw how we live here.

4 February 1996

Today my brother, Richard, called and thanked me for the magazine with his photograph of his quilt on the front and featured in the article. I think he was really proud, and so am I. I decided to tell him that Cynthia has suggested having a show in the U of M Gallery. He seemed to think this was a good idea and said that he would be glad to bring his wall hanging back for such a display. I will be thinking about it. Yes, I will think of a way to present them.

Tonight I worked on and finished my backs for the *Symphony* series. Some of the dyes have such exotic names nowadays that you can hardly guess what they are, and I had to mix them from primary colors—red, yellow, and blue—so I am especially proud of having been able to match up the colors in the silk to the colors on the front. I will say this again: *I may be at sea in some ways on these quilts, but I am proud of these backs!*

12 February 1996

Today my doctor's receptionist said she had seen the magazine cover and article at a friend's house. "When I saw it, I said, 'I know that woman!' " she told me. I felt a little embarrassed. I was calling about my medicine and the fact that I have lost twenty pounds this past year. The doctor's staff have always treated me with respect, but it feels wonderful to have something going on in my life that makes me more in their eyes than a patient with a chronic, disabling disease. My mother has been collecting the magazines from acquaintances, and they have called to congratulate her. My sister's friends have also asked for copies. Of course, I know that not all of these people are that impressed and, probably, some are rolling their eyes, but it has let me see Mother happy about something I have done, and for once, not just agonizing over my illness. Today I got a long letter from my uncle, Mother's oldest brother, who just had his eightieth birthday. He said he now has autographs from two famous people: mine on a small quilted item I made for him for his birthday and a postcard Charles A. Lindbergh had signed for him when he was eleven or twelve.

18 February 1996

I can now cut the heat down to sixty with weather outside in the teens and twenties. (Where the t's jump up in this paragraph, my hand has had muscle spasms. This worries me. My hand sometimes jerks pretty hard and I am not sure where this comes from. The medication? The oxygen? It bothers me especially when I am holding a cup of water or coffee and, naturally, spill it all over the place.)

21 February 1996

The other day we were watching a tape of Jodie's wedding and suddenly there was old FuFu, barking, of course. I felt such a pain and almost felt sick, I missed him so much. It does not make any sense, but this just happens. For years he slept with Eddie and me, and when Eddie got up around 5 a.m. to go to work, I would hold up the cover beside me, and he would snuggle into my bed and press up against me with his head on my arm, looking eyeball to eyeball. As strange as some people might find this, my heart still aches when I think about it. I never imagined that one day he would no longer be in my life—that I would live, and he would not. I still wish his death were just a bad dream, not reality.

I do hope I can get little Fu Two trained enough to bring him out into the den with me soon. His personality is very different from Fu's. I have to say he is a happier dog. He plays by himself. He doesn't bark. He loves going outside with Eddie. I want to be able to hold him, and I believe he will be an affectionate dog. I am glad Eddie got him for us, against my better judgment.

I am getting a lot done on my *Symphony*'s butterfly backs and am going back to the front sides this coming week.

2 March 1996

I can't believe it is March already. What difference does that make, you ask? I don't know, but I remember last time I was in the hospital, in Acute Care, there was a big clock and a calendar on the wall. We people on the fringes of life do mark time, for whatever reason, and the clock and calendar save the staff from some wear and tear, I suppose.

8 March 1996

This past weekend and early week were awful, minute by minute. I seriously wondered how much longer I could keep coughing. The muscles in my back and neck hurt so much I thought I could not

stand it anymore. If it were not for Eddie and the pain it would cause
him, and my Catholic roots, I think I would not have faced another
day. Eddie (who was kept awake with my coughing) kept telling me
I always get better and just to hang in there, and so I did. Now I have
a lot to do. I think I will stay in bed and sew after I pay some bills. I
want to call Susan, Cynthia's friend who trains dogs, to see if Fu Two
can be socialized. He is getting better about the biting, and that was
really worrying me.

Later. I want to add here that as I cut out the body of the butterfly I am attaching to the back of my *Symphony*, I realized it was made
from the heavy black cloth
Linda gave me before she died.
One night she drove over and
brought a sack of very nice cloth
that was left after she had made
some suits, blouses, and skirts for
work. It was very unexpected,
and after she died I wanted to
make some sort of memorial out
of these fabrics, though many of
them were too heavy to try to
quilt. I never got around to it
until tonight, but how fitting it
seems that the "exquisite butterflies" bodies in this *Symphony*
should be made out of cloth that

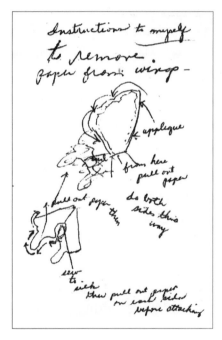

was probably used in a suit or jacket of Linda's. I wish sometimes
that it might be possible Linda and my grandmother and FuFu are in
some kind of spiritual world waiting for me. This seems childish, but
I think this helps hold back fear.

11 March 1996

I am trying to work more efficiently in order to complete some of my work. I have designed all the butterflies (six in all) for the reverse sides of *Symphony*, cut the paper templates from freezer paper, ironed them onto the batik fabrics, cut the fabric out, and then basted the fabric over the paper. After this, I put all the batik fabric in place on the black butterflies (previously cut out). And some have even been finished and the paper removed so that it looks like a print in the dark fabric. As I complete each butterfly, I will use the black dye on a Q-tip to blur the edges so they will appear without sharp edges on the silk. I want all of the backs to be as painterly as the fronts are linear. Just today, I think I figured out how to quilt little peaks and valleys in the silk to create a softer effect.

My mother's question has been nagging at me lately: "Do you mind if I ask what you are going to do with this stuff?" I have sometimes asked myself the same thing. But isn't the process what matters? I am not even able to see the product on most days. I cannot hold up the cloth very well or stand up for any length of time. Maybe I need to hire an assistant or reconsider that lung transplant. *Just kidding.* I tell Mother, "I'm an artist, and I appreciate your handing me that black fabric, even though you think I am crazy." A lot of artists are crazy. I was truly crazy once. Now I am only playing with Mother.

14 March 1996

One time, two days after she had made us a cheesecake and brought it by, Mother called to say she was coming right over to get the pan. I had really forgotten about it, though I had told her how good it was, and I didn't want her to know we hadn't eaten any yet. So as she was on her way over, I was trying to hide the cake, still in the pan, in the fridge. Suddenly I heard her say "Patsy" right behind me. My oxygen tubes had kept me from hearing her when she came in, and she startled me. I jumped, and the cake went flying into the back of the open refrigerator. I slammed the door, and later, when she was leaving and asked for the pan, I refused to give it to her.

Rather than tell her the truth and laugh it off, I just let her think I was being perverse. The stuff family conflicts are made of!

18 April 1996

I have stopped in the middle of sewing my dancing spirit onto my *Symphony's* back to write about what has been going on these days. I needed to come to this place, my journal, where I can admit that I am afraid. I have been feeling so bad this week that I even tried, unsuccessfully, to get home HealthCare to help me again. I wanted to write about my talk with Cynthia, this home health situation, and Eddie and my doctor. But now I find that I am too confused and tired to do this. I had all this to say while I was sewing and thought I would stop and pour out my heart, but now all at once I feel overwhelmed. I am going back to my sewing. It is going okay, and I feel so much better about it, working on it now.

4:00 a.m. I've gotten a lot done tonight; I've even pulled out two shades of silk ribbon to add as soon as my *spirit* is finished.

24 April 1996

I have been on a spiritual odyssey, you might say, for a very long time. And when I look deep inside myself, I see that I have been helped along in many different ways. I have an old prayer book (that belonged to my great-aunt) dated 1951, and on the very first page, I read, "A great sign appeared in heaven: A woman clothed with the sun, and the moon was under her feet, and upon her head a crown of twelve stars."—Apoc. 12:1. I am struck by this emphasis on

Pat's First Communion, Memphis, April 1951

the female expression of the divine and realize why our Protestant neighbor in Mississippi believed Catholics *worshiped* Mary. The way the nuns explained it to me was that we *honored* her. This female image of the Godhead, with its connection to nature and the universe, gives me great comfort.

26 April 1996

The other day I had this weird feeling that maybe Cynthia and I have created this third person whom the book is about. A person I might aspire to be, but feel too weak to be when I am up against tough situations.

27 April 1996

I have had an emotional upset, I guess you would say. Today I got two more pieces of mail, in addition to three letters earlier, questioning whether I qualify to have my insurance covering any more oxygen. As I read them, I felt the cold, icy fingers of fear squeezing my heart as they did when we were informed that our hospice benefits had run out, and before that, when we were handed a $6,000 hospital bill for care the insurance company considered unnecessary.

I am very, very grateful for all the good care I have received, but my doctor not calling us back, after our calls to him last week, has left me feeling abandoned or discarded and very frightened.

29 April 1996

Today I was greatly relieved to find out that the oxygen scare was all a mistake. The oxygen billing company assured me the whole fright was simply an error on their part.

3 May 1996

I wrote my doctor a letter today. I told him I felt like a doctorless patient who has been "care-managed" into the twilight zone.

It is 3:50 a.m. I need to write because I feel I may not make it much longer. I cannot stay with any task except for short stretches of time. The right side of my chest hurts off and on, and the left side feels as if it is crunching and popping for the first time. It was so wonderful to get Cynthia's letter. I had been planning to talk to her about the bad years and the hurt and the pain, my own and the pain of others who tried to help me. I wanted to write down directions to leave her for taking care of unfinished business so I could get through this last stage of illness calmly. It is an unbelievable coincidence that she has now written asking me to do this, to make my wishes known so I won't be worried.

I cannot write any more. Maybe later.

5 May 1996

My legs have begun to look awful: the same all the way down. I am always stooped in the tub so I have "rolls" at my midriff; but, anyway, Eddie dug out an old scale and I weighed 100 pounds. Now that's okay if you are a model, and I am short, but it just scared me. Since "fortyish," I have weighed 120 pounds, according to every hospital trip I have made. I came out of the seven-week killer trip to Baptist Hospital weighing 120. When I told Eddie that it was worrying me, he said he thought it was a good weight for me. Of course I did weigh around 115 pounds back when we met in 1971. He weighed 130! I am sure if this had happened when I was physically okay, I would have enjoyed clothes more. I could never stand anything tight around my waist. I have always had an odd figure (the mastectomy didn't help).

All three measurements were the same (or close). I am still irritated at Eddie. He says he knew he was not going to say the right thing, no matter what he said. Which is true. Something so intimate as weight sparks memories of how we see each other, or do not see each other. I think, here is this 56-year-old man helping his 53-year-old wife, with oxygen tubing on her ears and up her nose, in the tub. I think for him to survive all this he *cannot* allow himself to see, or worry about, weight, or any of this superficial stuff.

[In early June 1996, as it became harder for her to collect her thoughts, Pat finally closed her last journal and put it aside. From this point on, she used her surges of energy to scribble brief notes to herself and, every so often, short letters. These and my diary finish the record by carrying the threads of Pat's story through the summer and fall to a resting place.

Despite an early onset of fierce summer weather in Memphis, Pat assured me that she was still having some days when she could get back to her quilting, balance her checkbook, and walk to the bathroom fifteen feet from her bed. On June 9, with Eddie's help, she presided over the sorting of miscellaneous memorabilia, vestiges of the turbulent life she had put in storage two decades before. Seated behind a glass door that looked out on her carport, she watched anxiously as a couple of us excavated old letters, scrapbooks, and other souvenirs from a musty trunk Eddie had dragged from their storage shed. What we found was in much better shape than we feared. Lots of "Get Well" cards, many dating back to Pat's elementary school days, and a couple of letters to her from her father when he was away during World War II. Among several priceless photographs, one of her with her father when he was on leave showed him cradling her in his arms.

When I saw her again three weeks later, Pat looked much better and chuckled wickedly as she explained that she had been sparring with Eddie again, and yelling at him always seemed to revive her! The mood of the evening was mellow and our conversation flowed easily with serious talk about death and good-byes interspersed with silly discussions of clothes and embarrassing moments.

When I left, I took with me instructions that Pat had prepared so that others could finish the projects she could not complete: "Transfer fabric from these plastic bags and put them in folders." "Make charts to go by, using as a model the one I have left on the card table." Any novices who came forward to help "could do the machine-piecing over the basting," but "realistically," Pat suggested, it would probably be best "to let people swap jobs" and do what they wanted. Covered by webs of bracketed inserts and arrows, these notes bore the marks of her growing fatigue and disorientation.

Such visits were harder to manage as the summer wore on, however. For one thing, Pat's night-owl routine, never easy for daytime people, became more of a problem because she was sleeping so soundly that sometimes she slept until late afternoon, and it took her an hour or more to get fully alert. This effectively closed the door on us who could not get out in the evenings to see her. Her hearing had also become a serious barrier. When her coughing did not make her deaf, the gurgling and rush of oxygen through the tubes blocked out most of what others were saying. Being shut out of the conversations left her feeling worse when visitors came, more aware of her disadvantage and increasingly paranoid. Since the mail seemed the only way she could hold her own, she struggled to write a handful of letters during July and August.

A letter to me, dated August 14 and 15, had taken her two days to pull out of three scratched-out drafts, but removed any doubt that she was determined to see her own story through. To bring it to closure, she put in this letter a piece of self-portraiture that she suggested might serve as a metaphor for her finale: a picture of herself poised on the cusp between fading night and the coming day:

"I go to sleep at daybreak, now. Others are just waking up as I

close my eyes. One morning recently, I watched the sun rise. Through a small opening in the blinds, I watched the watercolor sky pour its wash over the day unfolding. I said a morning prayer, as I've started to do now as I go to sleep. And I realized what a strange life I have had—never stranger than now—because I have tried to live it on my own terms.

"My life has taken me on an unexpected journey. In my later years, as I've searched for means to express my feelings, it feels as if I have poured all my passion for life into my work. I have discovered much about texture and deep, bright color that sings, and I have explored the power of light and how it can bring things together.

"I saw where I wanted my spirit to go, and I am going there. Some days I feel very close to the end of my long search and discovery. My hope is that I will go soundly to sleep when the time comes. This is everyone's wish, I believe. I have to trust that I can get through whatever happens with grace."

Her final scene was still off in the future, however. A month later, she was writing of trying to get back to work on her two quilts-in-progress, despite her rough days, and the fact that her hands were no longer steady enough. "I keep thinking I will divide up my day between them," she wrote me in late September, "but on bad days I get nothing done and on better days I try to catch up with my relatives or friends." She was also putting her business in order, she said, not only leaving directions concerning her "quilt stuff"— how she wanted to have her unfinished work completed by other quilters—but leaving directions about how she wished to be cared for if she become helpless: no hospitalization under any circumstances, no heroic intervention. She did not want to leave haphazard instructions that "bounce around and nobody knows what was really intended," she said emphatically. If she could get something *on paper, "then you would know, as I would, whatever needs to be stated clearly."*

In early October, the Clines were again accepted for hospice care, resuming the helpful relationship of two years before. Back then, Pat's survival past six months had ended "terminal" status; she had been reassessed "stable" and dropped from the program. Now she was thirty pounds lighter and so frail and weary that nurses who knew her before were startled.

When I went to see Pat on the afternoon of October 8, I found her asleep. So I sat in a chair by her bed and, surrounded by family photographs on the walls, visited once again with the people whom I had met in the journals. Then, on the nightstand, where colored pencils and spools of thread mingled with medications, I spotted an envelope bearing my name. It contained a letter, the last Pat would write me, in which she said that she finally knew how the artist's story would end. She could no longer quilt; she was simply too tired and now she would hand the work over to us.]

PART III:
IN THE
STUDIO

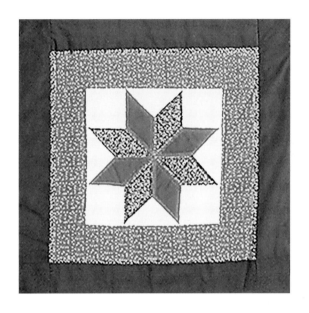

Pat in her studio, August 1995

PART III: IN THE STUDIO

Patricia Cline carried her studio with her for almost a dozen years. From the fall of 1981, when she joined a beginning quilters' class, to the early 1990s, when she was no longer leaving her home, Pat rarely went out unaccompanied by an oversize cotton tote bag with everything needed to work on transportable sections of projects. Fishing out templates and piecework, she set up her shop whenever she found a spare moment and somewhere to sit and spread out as she made her rounds: in friends' and relatives' kitchens and living rooms, auto mechanics' garages, doctors' offices, hospital rooms, or the car on long trips to the beach with young nieces. When an oxygen tank and tubes reined her in, the artist anchored her workplace at home, in an extra bedroom, filling it with her fabrics, books, ironing board, sewing machine, and other paraphernalia. Here she also created an archives by converting a daybed into an oversize horizontal file where sketches, work notes, and patterns were stored in layers by project, and covered with a spread. Eventually the few steps to this workroom became so exhausting that the artist's world underwent a further consolidation, until her hospital bed in the den—surrounded by storage bins, ironing board, and tables—became her live-in studio. Over the sixteen years, in the work space that changed as Cline's life was changing, the artist produced a body of ever more challenging concepts that stretched her skills, imagination, and daring. Though most of the works have long since left home as gifts, they can still be seen on the studio walls that come into focus as we go back to learn how each piece was created.

Sampler Quilt

(1981–82) 89 ¹/₂" x 110 ¹/₂"

THE ARTIST'S FIRST PIECE was a "sampler quilt," conceived as a Christmas gift for her mother, Mary Margaret "Bea" Roberts, and finished early in 1982. This bright and expansive bedcover started more modestly as a learning device in Cline's first quilting class, where she and her classmates made 18" x 18" blocks to master the rudi-

mentary piecing techniques and acquaint themselves with a repertoire of basic quilting designs: Cathedral Window, Grandmother's Flower Garden, Dresden Plates, Trapunto Butterfly, Eight-pointed Star, and Log Cabin. Impatient to get past this practice stage and have something to show for her diligence, Cline worked out a plan for making a full-fledged quilt from her lap-size sample squares. She made more than one block in each of these six patterns—four appear twice in the quilt—so that she would have enough to practice on before putting the best in her *Sampler.* As is common with serious quilters, Cline washed all of the dozens of pieces to guard against fading and shrinkage before she assembled the top.

Cline recruited her sisters to make another ten blocks. Though none of them quilted, all had done counted cross-stitch embroidery, and they used this technique to work flower motifs into loosely woven Aida cotton. Cline did the piecework, added the borders, and quilted the top to the batting and back. The bold and unusual use of primary colors, which presaged more daring experiments later, won the high praise of her teacher, Marilyn Califf, who said the *Sampler* was one of the best of its kind she had ever seen.

Women's Voices

(1983–84) 48"x 48"

WHEN CLINE'S NEXT CONSTRUCTION appeared in 1984, it announced that her recent return to college and serious study of art had aroused an incipient feminist sensibility. Cline had been learning about such neglected artists as Rosa Bonheur, Berthe Morisot, Käthe Kollwitz,

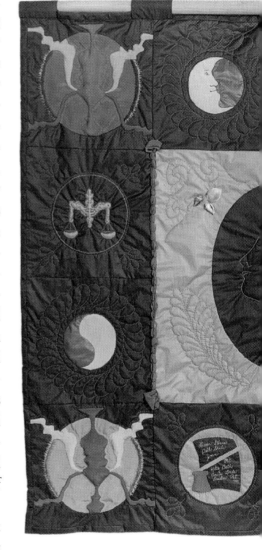

and Mary Cassatt, whose work showed that boldness of line, strong images, and heroic themes were by no means gender specific. In the notebooks she kept for art history classes, Cline now was lodging complaints and challenging the disparaging distinctions between so-called "high" and "low" art forms, which placed women's work below men's and diminished techniques and traits deemed *feminine*. "In the category of *low art*," Cline mimicked the experts, "we find 'domestic handicraft produced by commercial artists, women, peasants, and savages'; at least this is the opinion of the culture's most influential voices. But what of the many respected male artists whose work has exhibited *feminine* traits?" It seemed to her that any scheme that described art as either all male or all female was artificial and not of much value.

With her second quilt, a 48" x 48" hanging of soft polished chintz in brown, sage, and heather, Cline moved her rebuttal from her notebooks onto a larger, more public page. The pattern, the first Cline designed by herself, grew out of the Women's Voices course where

208

during the spring of 1983, she had read for the first time Virginia Woolf's novel *To the Lighthouse* and Alice Walker's new book, *The Color Purple*, where quilting is used to suggest how women's bonding can heal broken lives and build strong, creative communities.

Emboldened by artists like these to make herself present in what she created, Cline embroidered as her quilt's centerpiece a large woman's face modeled after her own. She framed it with rows of quilting stitches that etched in organic designs, and then she attached some real seashells, pulling further into relief the connections between the natural world and women's creativity. On the twelve outside blocks, smaller emblems pay tribute to some of the female artists and writers she had studied and to the principles they promoted through their work. A diminutive tower over a swatch of blue sea alludes to Woolf's *To the Lighthouse* and its illumination of the artist's task. Elsewhere, the pan scales of justice, the waning moon, and the yin-yang symbol reiterate Woolf's ideal of balance and harmony. On the corners, Cline worked in four stylized butterflies to acknowledge Judy Chicago's call for strong female imagery and a recognition of women's achievements. Finally, at the lower left, Cline embroidered a small manuscript page with her name and those of her classmates in the Women's Voices course.

Sunrise Yellow Noise

(1981–89) 88 $^1/_2$" x 78 $^1/_2$"

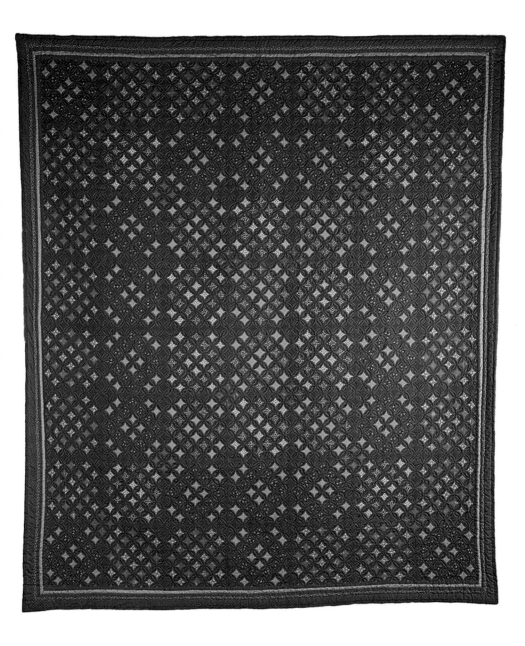

CLINE'S QUICKNESS TO BREAK with tradition in order to put her own stamp on her work had been evident even before she began *Women's Voices* in 1983. Two years earlier, as a gift for her husband, she had started a much more ambitious—and tedious—project, that gave the familiar Cathedral Window pattern a highly unorthodox treatment. Actually, while enough like a quilt to be treated as part of the genre—and to win a blue ribbon at the 1989 Mid-South Fair Quilt Show—Cathedral Windows are not, strictly speaking, quilted constructions. Instead of three layers of top, back, and batting connected and held firm by deep quilting stitches, the padded effect is produced by joining small squares—the little "windows" inside the large one—each folded into itself to make its own padding. Traditionally, the Cathedrals have been made on a white muslin background with the windows' different colors in a more or less random arrangement, but Cline chose to do something she never saw anywhere. She used a dark background against which she worked out a carefully balanced mosaic, a large radiating design that draws the eye from shadow around the outside to a core of glowing light.

While the cost of this project in patience and time often seemed to Cline so exorbitant she vowed "never again," the investment of so many hours of labor over seven years was more than repaid as the artist's relationship to her creation evolved, transforming them both. On the technical level, this slow evolution gave Cline a chance to refine such difficult treatments as the strip-pieced, mitered corners. It also allowed her to work out several color problems by showing them to her friends in her quilting guild. On one member's suggestion, she replaced some of the earth brown with sky blue in ten constellations of windows, achieving the effect of a heavenly vision.

The composition's interior meanings changed over time, too, as the work became a chronicle of her personal journey. As if every feeling and memory that had visited her as she sat slowly stitching had left its mark, Cline could read in the piecework the history of her unexpected setbacks early in life and her equally unexpected successes in college and married life later. "When I started out, I was just as confident that this quilt would follow my plan as I had been about the course of my life when I was young," she reflected. "I carefully planned it. I drew out the entire design before the first stitch was made." But at the last minute, changing a single color "created a different quilt." Her art, like her story, had taken its own direction.

By the time Cline added the borders and binding, her symbolism had clarified: this Cathedral Window, she said, embodies the window of time during which, through hard work and patience, she managed to make her escape from darkness to light. Despair and self-loathing and hopelessness were all behind her. She felt reborn, redeemed, and at peace with herself. "I knew," she later recalled, "whatever happened, I had proved to myself I had worth, and that I could endure."

Cline found her title for this celebration of earthly striving and triumph in a nineteenth-century poem called "Country Burial" by Emily Dickinson. A poet who frowned on a longing for heaven that spurned the good life here and now, Dickinson likened this outlook to leaving a comfortable bed unused until time for death's sleep, or to closing the blinds to keep out the world's warmth and beauty. With *Sunrise Yellow Noise* Cline created a quilt for the bed of life and not for a resting place in a dark chamber visited only by death.

Cline's idea of creating her next three pieces, a trio of wall hangings for her three sisters, emerged in the fall of 1987—after some routine lab tests in Memphis had seemed to show cancer in her lungs, and after a second opinion at the Mayo Clinic sent her home with a different and better prognosis. The scare of this false alarm and the real, accelerating decline in her health had forced her to face her mortality as she had not done before. "Even though I had dealt with chronic illness for a very long time, my husband and I went through the same upheaval as anyone else when handed an absolute death sentence," Cline explained later. Spurred to put her accounts in order, she turned to art to complete an appropriate legacy for her family.

Through this difficult period, Cline's sisters had put their own problems aside to let her know that they cared and would help. She wanted to make quilts for them, as she had for her mother and husband. Cline started all three at the same time and kept them going simultaneously to guard against any appearance of favoritism. She also involved all the sisters in the planning, "which led to a lot of fabric and sketches being mailed back and forth." Katie and Mary Jo, or "Jodie," chose traditional patterns, while Anne was receptive to something more unusual.

Introspect

(1987–91) 36" x 36"

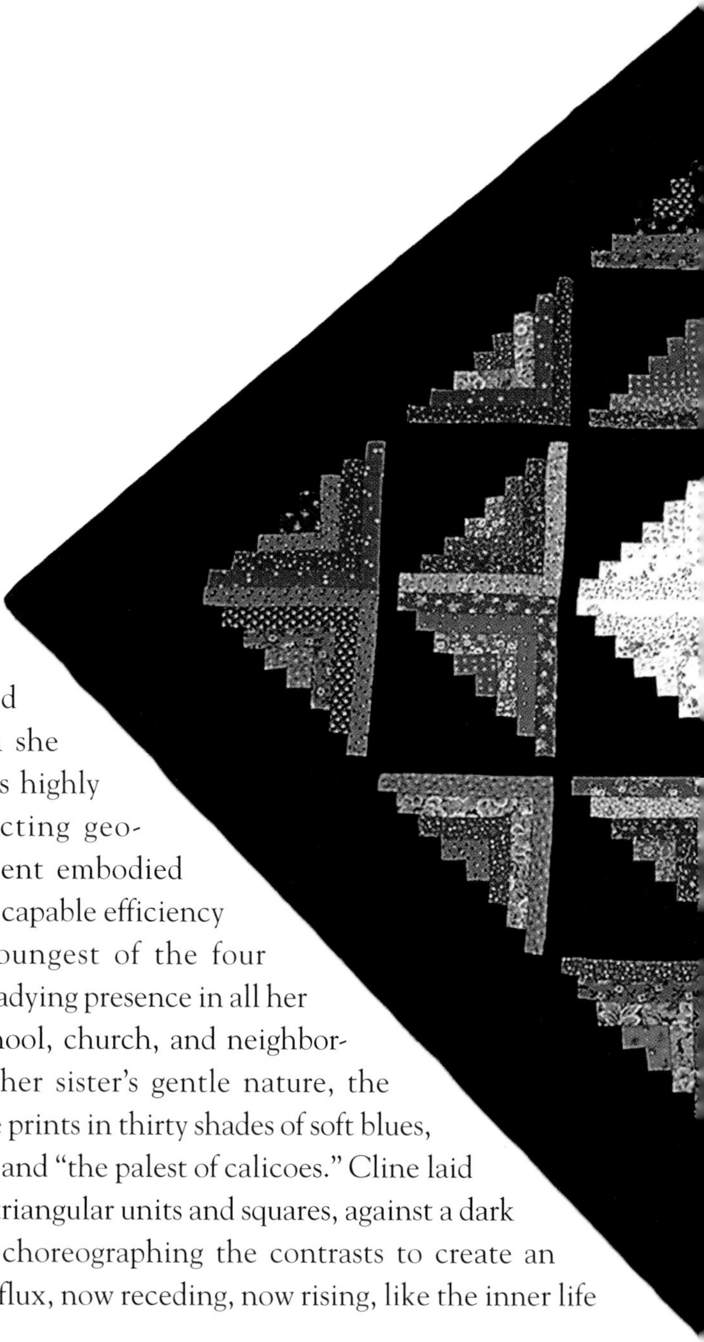

FOR KATIE,
Cline fashioned a
small, strip-pieced
Log Cabin, which she
called *Introspect*. Its highly
complex and exacting geo-
metrical arrangement embodied
the orderliness and capable efficiency
that made this youngest of the four
Roberts sisters a steadying presence in all her
circles—family, school, church, and neighborhood. To capture her sister's gentle nature, the
artist chose delicate prints in thirty shades of soft blues,
mauves, and pinks, and "the palest of calicoes." Cline laid
out these colors in triangular units and squares, against a dark
navy background, choreographing the contrasts to create an
illusion of layers in flux, now receding, now rising, like the inner life

214

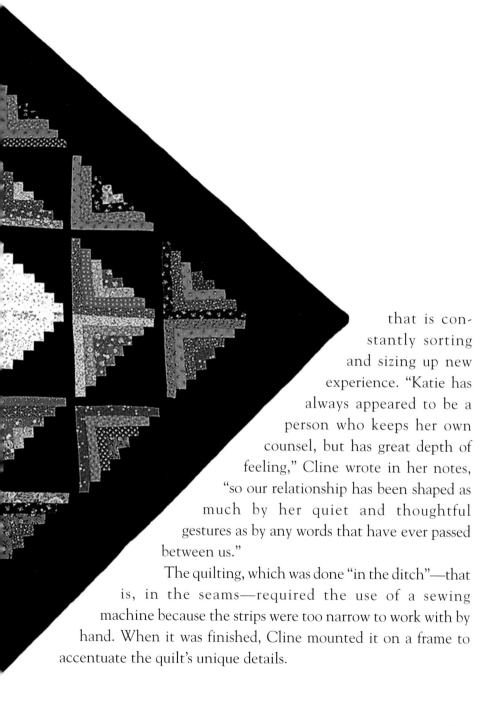

that is con-
stantly sorting
and sizing up new
experience. "Katie has
always appeared to be a
person who keeps her own
counsel, but has great depth of
feeling," Cline wrote in her notes,
"so our relationship has been shaped as
much by her quiet and thoughtful
gestures as by any words that have ever passed
between us."

The quilting, which was done "in the ditch"—that
is, in the seams—required the use of a sewing
machine because the strips were too narrow to work with by
hand. When it was finished, Cline mounted it on a frame to
accentuate the quilt's unique details.

Sisters

(1987–1991) 35" x 45"

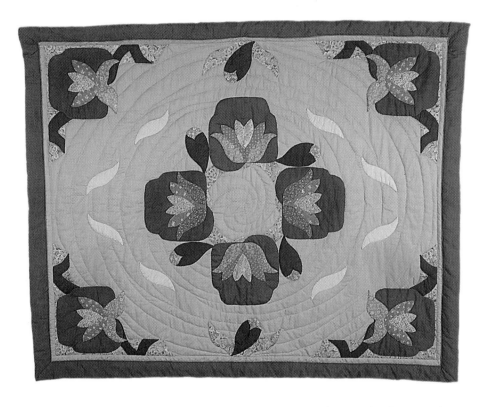

CLINE WAS REMINDED almost as soon as she worked out a plan for Mary Jo's quilt that an artist's creation invariably acquires a mind of its own. Here the artist's initial intent was to show how the fabric and thread of two lives had been intertwined in a way that made their bond self-contained and unique. But once the work started to move along, she saw that this bond was more complicated and needed a much more inclusive and flexible syntax. The special ties that bound her to Jodie could not be detached from the larger web of connections that held all four sisters together in an ever shifting, sometimes uneasy, but no less sacred and cherished intimacy.

"At first I called this piece *Love*," the artist recalled after finishing it, the name having come from a line in a song called "The Rose": *"I say love, it is a flower, and you its only seed …"* Yet as she worked on the pattern, she started to see it not as a single large flower, but as a circle of four connected lilies afloat on the water of life. They touched when the currents drew them together, and at other times drifted to their separate corners of the world. Forever redefining themselves in relation to the group, all were vital to their constellation's design. In her family, Cline mused, as she added the finishing touches in 1991, the females seemed to have had a hard time seeing themselves as individuals independent of these relationships. This had not been the case with her brother. "He seems to have known who he is all along, or perhaps, being male, he has simply not felt as free as his sisters to confess to his doubts and confusion."

For this compact appliquéd hanging, the artist adapted a pattern she saw on a large spread, and put her signature on it by using original colors and quilting designs: a palette of blue, rose, and white, and spirals suggestive of swirling water. Deceptive in its simplicity, the design's execution was difficult. To give her stylized water lilies the substance she wanted, Cline had to build up the appliqués with extra layers of fabric, as many as six in some places. The quilting, also exacting, had to be stitched from the center out, and in oval and circular patterns, to give the effect of the sisters' drifting or pulling away from the others, only to be pulled back by the primary ties of their sisterhood. Only after she finished this project did Cline discover that the use of lilies to represent the creative life forces that keep families strong is a symbolism that goes back at least as far as early Egypt.

Ascending Phoenix

(1987–91) 43" x 52"

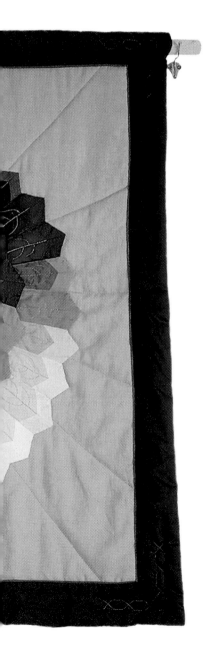

CLINE CONSIDERED THE QUILT she created for Anne, the sister closest to her in age, to be more creative and technically ambitious than anything she had attempted. It was also the most overtly autobiographical. Cline's friends and family could readily grasp the meaning of its dominant figure, the fabulous three-eyed bird of rebirth, and understand why the artist identified with it. They knew, without reading her notes, that she wished to consign to her cloth her feelings of freedom and hope in the aftermath of her cancer scare. Her reprieve at the Mayo Clinic, which felt like a gift from above, had awakened the artist's desire to know and make peace with the source. This quilt for her sister was also a record of Cline's pledge to search for God.

Cline's central image had come to her almost mystically, she later recalled. She had sat herself down on the floor with fabrics spread out around her, a ritual she used regularly to open her inner eye, and as she did, she "saw a beautiful phoenix rising again from the ashes." Certain that this was the emblem she wanted, she researched the bird's mythological

219

meanings. Associated by name with the Greek god of healing and sacred among the Egyptians, the phoenix stood for rebirth and renewal in both early Christian and pagan cultures. "In Christianity, the Phoenix typifies Christ," her research revealed, "so this would fit in with Anne, a nurse and a good Christian in the truest sense: an unselfish person."

Cline faced her phoenix forward with its head slightly turned to the side and its crescent wingspan turned upward to represent her yearning to know and be one with the source of new life. She built the bird's body from "prairie points"—small squares folded into Vs—arranging them so the earth tones, splashes of blue, and leafy patterns grew warmer and richer as they moved up. Her working notes acknowledge the Japanese as the inspiration for this motley wardrobe. They fashioned their phoenix to represent the entire universe, "with its back signifying the crescent moon; its wings, the wind; its feet, the earth; its tail, trees and plants." To carry the viewer's eye up and along the arch of the massive wings, she attached six blue feathers with metallic embroidery thread.

Rising out of the appliquéd flames, the phoenix is resurrected against a background of soft, ashlike fabric, a blend of fibers rarely used in quilting because they are very hard to manage—but perfect for what she meant to convey. To suggest a release from earthly fetters, Cline tried to create the illusion that the appliquéd bird was not stitched to the cloth but free to take flight, and in this she believed she had succeeded. "It looked as if it could actually be lifted off the background," she boasted, imagining her viewers furtively reaching out and pulling the fabric gently to see if their eyes could be trusted. On this ashen field, she did the quilting in radiating rows of stitches to represent rays of energy and the pulsating forces of new creation coming from higher, ultimate sources of power.

On the deepest level, the physical work and contemplative time that went into this project acquired a sacramental significance for the artist. As she transformed her limp fabric into a powerful figure of life and rebirth, one that emerges out of the flames with magnificent wings raised in benediction, she felt that she was performing a ritual act of consecration and prayer. "As I worked on it into the night," Cline recalled, "it provided me with a sense of renewal this year. This quilt is about rebirth and immortality." She was so proud of how it turned out that she used a reproduction of it as her hallmark on the brochure for her first show at Meristem Bookstore.

Flowers on the Wall

(1990–91) 35" x 35"

FLOWERS ON THE WALL, A DISARMING floral arrangement in rose, mauve, and dusty pink, got its start as a learning project in a stained-glass quilting workshop that Cline's guild attended during the spring of 1990. But predictably, this hanging, the first Cline created to keep, ended up as more than an exercise. As the artist developed her velvety brushed-cotton flowers and shiny polished leaves, and appliquéd the narrow black strips that outline each section to look like stained glass, she was also stitching in a private mythology about the bonds that connect generations of women. By the time she was ready to finish this piece by adding a cable border, she could read in its stylized contours a timeless story about how three women of different ages—much like herself, her mother, and her grandmothers—could inspire and strengthen each other, but also pass on their pain and passivity. As women observe their elders, she wrote as she thought of her own southern legacy, they frequently turn into "soft-spoken flowers" that hide their thorns beneath their bright leaves and velvet petals. The trick, she said, is in learning how to embrace and how to let go without anyone's getting hurt.

Enlightenment

(1989–91) 86" x 68"

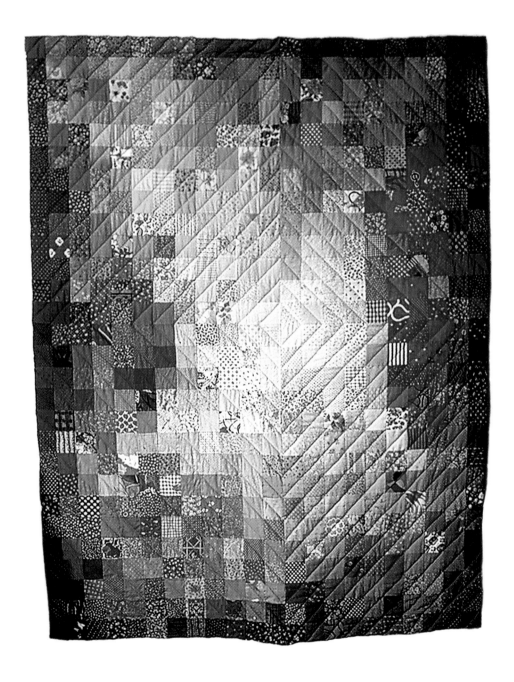

ENLIGHTENMENT IS A UNIQUE ADAPTATION of the popular Charm Quilt tradition, where tops are constructed from small pieces cut with a single pattern from different fabrics, no two of which are the same. Cline had no idea how hard it would be to find all the pieces for the six hundred three-inch-square blocks her ambitious design required, nor did she expect to be compensated as well as she was, or as promptly. Yet long before she had the pleasure of finishing off the quilt and hearing it praised, she began to reap a greater reward in feeling a bond with the past. "When I was at my mother's one weekend, I rummaged about and found some real treasures in a cedar chest, remnants that were, quite literally, *the pieces of a past we had shared:* fabric from yellow chintz curtains, children's dresses, blouses, and shirts." Cline's mother and grandmother "spent many hours together getting us children ready to go back to school or dressing 'angels' and 'flowers' for plays and parades." As she worked with these relics, the artist could feel the presence of these older women and their passion for sewing.

While it took several years for the artist to gather the number of pieces she needed, it did not take long for her overall vision to clarify. Cline decided to have a prism of colors, with the darkest on the outer edges and palest on the inside, and arrange them to make it appear that a radiant light was shining out through the center. By quilting her pieced top against a black backing in rippling diamond designs, she intensified the illusion of movement into the center and represented her faith that she would discover the light if she honestly made the effort. She had been inspired, she later said, by some words that the fourteenth-century monk Fra Giovanni had left on a wall of a cave: "There is a radiance and glory in the darkness ... To see, we have only to look." So clear was this message that, as Cline patiently pieced this large quilt, the act of shifting and rearranging the small blocks felt like a rite by which she was working her way from the darkest shades of hopelessness to the light of understanding and inner peace.

Environmental Concerns

(1990–91) 63" x 52"

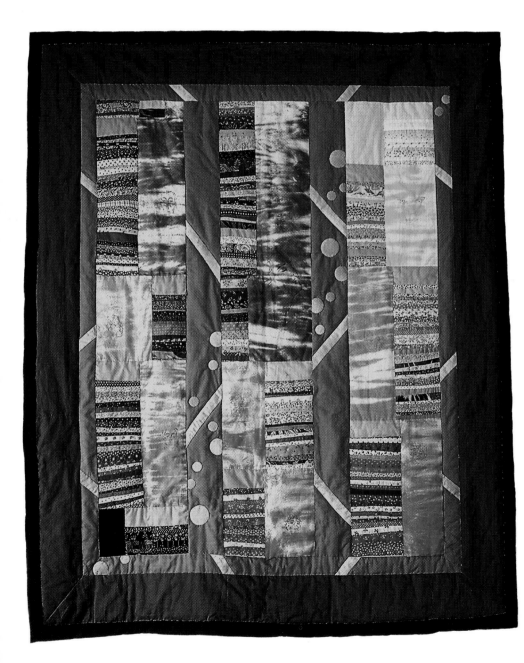

WHEN THE ARTIST COMPLETED *Environmental Concerns* in 1991 and presented it to Meristem, a new woman's bookstore in midtown Memphis, the freedom of her design and boldness of her palette showed how far she had come in the past seven years toward finding her voice as an artist and woman. This gift to the store that offered her space for her first public, one-woman show was a telling contrast to Cline's 1983–84 *Women's Voices*. Granted, that earlier work had shown something of Cline's disobedient nature, her tendency to balk at instructions and willingness to pay for the freedom to set her own rules. There her choice of glazed chintz, which experienced quilters avoid because it is so hard to handle, turned out to be more than she had bargained for, but she stuck by her decision. Daring, too, especially in the Mid-South, where quilters were likely to be more conservative, were her allusions to Judy Chicago's erotic and controversial butterflies, emblems included to recognize the radical wing of feminist art. Yet in 1983, the novice quilter had not been ready to make any radical break with tradition, and worked her innovations within a familiar grid of large, uniform blocks and kept her colors subdued. By contrast, when seven years later Cline set out to make her hanging for Meristem, she had no qualms about replacing conventional structures with her own, using a palette of strong, almost arrogant colors.

At the "soul" of *Environmental Concerns*, Cline explained in a letter to Meristem's owners, she put all the pain that she felt when she saw how much women are hurt by the fears and myths that poison our culture. Undervalued and misunderstood in the past, her sex had been edited out of the annals, as if they were not worth mentioning, and here toward the end of the twentieth century, most of the world's women still were not valued as full human beings.

Oppressive social systems kept them from feeling their personal power and using it. The worst part of this, Cline went on, was that women are so firmly "stitched into their environment" that it is hard for them to detach themselves from its virulent misogyny. They can no

Sketches for embroidered faces on Environmental Concerns

longer see their own worth or each other's, or pool their strength to form a cohesive sisterhood. It troubled the artist to see that even some self-described feminists lacked the skills or desire to work together. Surely, she said, the contamination that undermined female collaboration is as worthy of our concern as the poisons that threaten our natural world.

To express this, Cline started *Environmental Concerns* by piecing together small calico strips and larger swatches of hand-dyed and air-brushed fabrics until she had built three vertical panels connected with longer, diagonal strips. These represent the prisons of fear and ignorance that block women's empowerment. Next, she embroidered six barely visible faces of imprisoned women, society's prisoners, who are cut off from us in their solitary cells behind the walls. In the background are appliquéd patches of smoke-streaked sky and bubbles of poisonous gas. The artist stitched five of the faces with closed eyes, but not giving into despair, she allowed the sixth to peer out at us from the bright block of gold at the quilt's upper left, letting her glance meet ours like a ray of hope. In the same spirit, she used metallic thread to animate the faces. After she finished this quilt, Cline kept hearing the words of Alice Walker, who wrote of invisible women being like "exquisite butterflies trapped in an evil honey … their striving spirits [seeking] to rise, like frail whirlwinds from the hard red clay." And so she borrowed the quilt back and added some butterflies, whose sparkling wings lift them over the border and out of one corner at the top.

Julie's Quilt
(1991–93) 39" x 59"

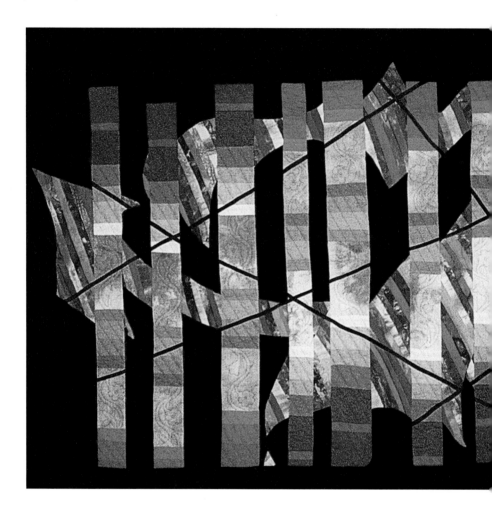

SHORTLY AFTER HER SHOW AT MERISTEM in the spring of
1991, Cline began a collaborative project with her sister Anne's
younger daughter, Julie Meiman, then a college freshman in Memphis. Cline's recent triumph and public acclaim had awakened in
Julie not only the pride of kinship, but also a yearning to make quilts
herself and continue this family tradition. Since she intended to
stay in the city to work that summer, it seemed like an ideal time to

learn from her aunt. The artist, for her part, welcomed this chance to shore up the bond between them and proposed that they make a small quilt together.

Cline's initial thought was to have a design that captured her niece's free-spirited nature. Her aunt saw her then as the happy-go-lucky young woman who still was as given to giggling playfully as she was when, as a little girl, her Uncle Eddie and Aunt Patsy took her to ride on the merry-go-round at the fair. Julie wanted her aunt to be in the quilt with her to preserve their times together.

The design they came up with was anchored by Julie's initials, JCM, with the C standing also for Cline. Cut in stylized shapes drawn so freely outsiders have trouble deciphering them, the letters were then encoded under a grid of black ribbon and bright fabric strips, which carry the eye up and down like the notes on a musical staff or a carousel's horses. These elements crisscross to form what the aunt and her niece referred to as "windows," openings onto the ground of their special relationship. In the private places behind these windows, the quilters created an interplay of bold linear panels and subtle curved movement by stitching an almost invisible S-shaped motif: a vine with three flowers to show that their bond was actually part of a triad that also included Anne, Julie's mother. The flowers in the windows were

Julie's idea, a way to remember Cline's vintage of "hippies and flower children" in the 1960s. The two quilters also collaborated in dyeing some fabric—not only to learn the technique, but as a sacramental act that strengthened their ties to past generations of women who worked with textiles and color.

Cline's notes and journal entries show that she researched and chose her colors for their psychological impact more than to satisfy personal taste. She selected her reds and pinks to convey Julie's youth and romantic or passionate nature. The yellows speak of Julie's optimism and warmth.

Sketch of flowers in the windows of Julie's Quilt

Cline started out thinking this quilt should be called "Carousel" or "Calliope" because of its carefree associations, which seemed a good match with Julie's nature. But by the time Cline was ready to put on the four-inch black border and sign their names, Julie's travels abroad had opened her girlish eyes to some of life's harsh realities. In Africa she witnessed the carnage and suffering of the Rwandans, and in Japan, the horrors let loose when a terrorist cult released deadly nerve gas on a train. She arrived home more serious—cheerful, but no longer quite as free and exuberant. Julie's music tempered, the carousel now seemed too frivolous an emblem for her. So the hanging was registered simply as *Julie's Quilt.* It was the first, Cline noted, that she produced consciously "for the next generation of women" so they would have "something of us" to take with them into the next century.

Fans from the Past : Variation 1
78" x 64"

Pieced c. 1930s –1940s by Dora Nix Gillespie Rutledge and Nellie Gillespie Roberts

Fans from the Past: Variation 2
86" x 62"

Pieced c. 1930s –1940s by Dora Nix Gillespie Rutledge and Nellie Gillespie Roberts

NO SOONER HAD CLINE SENT off *Julie's Quilt* than she found herself part of another collaboration, one that bridged a yet greater divide between women of different eras. This project entailed the repair and quilting of two bed-size tops, both pieced in the same traditional pattern, Fans from the Past, by her paternal great-grandmother, Dora Nix Gillespie Rutledge, and her grandmother, Nellie Gillespie Roberts, half a century earlier. Several generations of women had handed them down until they were put in Cline's hands by her mother in 1993. Cline could see from the sometimes dissonant colors that these tops were functional pieces, not works of art, but because they were now treasured heirlooms, she included her restoration in her inventory of serious art.

Cline knew that these tops deserved quilting if only because the fabric documents women's Depression-era resourcefulness. In those difficult times and into the war years, the need to make do inspired producers to sell their flour in printed cotton sacks that housewives could use to make quilts and small garments. As she reinforced or replaced the frayed stitches, the artist could still see the tracks of small holes that were left in the fabric when her grandmother's mother removed the heavy thread of the seams. After Cline washed and repaired the piecework and added some suitable borders, she sent them out for a commercial jobber to quilt by machine. Though she knew very little about this woman from rural Tennessee, the work of restoring her quilts brought back memories of a small, wrinkled lady alone in her room, barely able to see, but still doing the work her fingers had learned by heart. Some of the segments that make up the fans have as many as six tiny pieces in them, and if they were not "on the mark (as handiwork goes)," the great-granddaughter noted defensively, "they were awfully good for someone who more than likely was in her nineties and nearly blind at the time she put them together. I have her earlier quilts with their perfect craftsmanship," Cline pointed out, protecting the woman whose hand she felt guiding her own.

Georgia on My Mind
(1991–94) 50" x 61"

IN 1991, WHEN THE ARTIST'S brother and sister-in-law came from Texas to see her Meristem show and the quilts she had made for her mother and sisters, Cline realized her work was still "far from finished," her family's legacy still incomplete, because she had yet to make something for Richard and Carol. This became her next project, and three years later, she sent them her gift, *Georgia on My Mind*. Rich in symbolism, its text can be read on several different levels.

Here Cline's intent was to celebrate the low-keyed camaraderie she believed she shared with Richard and Carol because of their similar values and temperaments. As with her and Eddie, her brother and sister-in-law had no children, but did have two dogs and a huge affection for animals. Both were also serious artists: he a wildlife photographer, she a printmaker who had a job in computer animation. Their passion for nature and independence—they were building a house themselves near a national wildlife reserve in Texas—were also qualities Cline could identify with and wished to incorporate. At the same time, and more profoundly, she wanted to use this project to look at her own solitude, which, hard as it was, had been crucial to her art and spiritual journey. She wished to evoke the ambiguity of the present moment—a transitional time when, approaching death, she was passing through an "internal wilderness."

Cline found her point of departure for this symbolic text in a desert painting by Georgia O'Keeffe, *Ram's Head with Hollyhock*. In that 1935 study, the skull of a ram with long, sinuous horns and a flower, both starkly realistic, appear in the foreground as if suspended in air. In the lower background along the horizon, O'Keeffe painted a row of low hills, whose mounds of hard clay speak of thousands of years of erosion by wind and rain. Above the red and gold of the hills, dotted with spots of green brush, the sky is entirely covered with gray and white storm clouds. O'Keeffe explained that by using the skull, she was trying to "pare away the unessential" so as to reveal the harsh beauty of natural process. This was also a part of Cline's purpose, so she made a ram's skull her focal point, using trapunto to sculpt and shade and give the design dimension by padding small sections and pulling them into relief. She also ran a long strip of desert along the bottom to evoke O'Keeffe's Southwest, where Richard and Carol were building their home and where Carol made sculptures from skulls. From this point on, Cline composed her own statement about nature's rhythm and mysteries.

Like O'Keeffe, who said that the bones that she painted were not meant as symbols of death but of process, Cline used the desert and ram's skull to mark her long path from an earthbound consciousness to the realm of the spirit. To direct this movement, she added a black-and-white crane in flight at the quilt's upper right, dressing its appliquéd body in real iridescent feathers—to cover an application of dry brush paint that failed to bring out the contours. This figure, which is "just about to disappear" off the border, is an unstable symbol—in some cultures standing for long life, in others, impending extinction. Here it embodies, Cline wrote, the full range of complex emotions attached to the cycles of life and death.

At the heart of the piece, behind the skull and the crane, a desert sky of hand-dyed fabric animates every other element. Its spectrum of colors extends from the ominous blues and browns of a threatening storm to radiant and benedictory deep rose and violets from which a gold light breaks through from a higher source. Cline's quilting sometimes creates long rays of light that stream down to the desert, and sometimes follows the path of the crane's flight, infusing waves of energy into the undulating sky. While conceding this scene might as easily be a sunset as a sunrise, and that this, like all art, is open to interpretation, Cline preferred to think of it as "the gift of another new day, as yet another fresh chance to set things right."

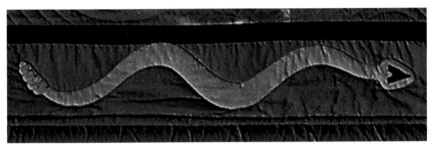

Detail of snake on border of Georgia on My Mind

On the borders of this desert quilt, the artist appliquéd two gold snakes and two rows of yellow "flying geese," the latter an old quilt motif using cloth deftly folded into small triangles. More than ornamental, these emblems, Cline wrote, are her way of expressing the need for "a wiser, more mystical concept of animals." Their world was older and more complete than ours and in some ways far more evolved than we ever imagined. If they were not brothers and sisters of ours, they were not our underlings either. "They are other nations, caught with ourselves in the net of life and time," Cline wrote, repeating the words of an unknown author. Ultimately, they were "fellow prisoners of the splendor and travail of the earth."

Victorian Echo

(1990–) projected size 96" x 78"

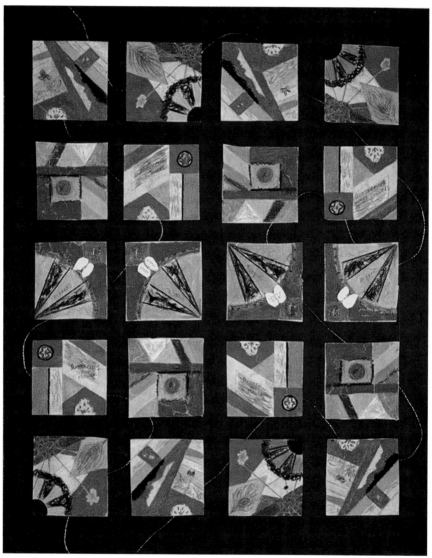

Mock-up in colored pencil on tissue, mounted on poster board, metallic gold thread overlay

"TO CONTAIN THE MADNESS" in cultures where women are treated like decorative objects was Cline's stated purpose when, during the fall of 1990, she started an oversize quilt that adapted the late-nineteenth-century fashion of "crazy work." That fad was suddenly all the rage once again a century later, and Cline's adaptation both celebrated and criticized it. This quilt was a way of thanking the feminists, whose prodding had helped her to see her worth and make the most of her talents. Cline was also glad for the recognition this vogue brought to women who understood that beautiful things can strengthen us spiritually. But she had reservations about this needlework's lavish display of surface embellishments. She saw the mood of nostalgia surrounding the latest Victorian fad as a dangerous retreat from the progress of women in recent decades. The fondness for obsolete styles was eroding the feminist thought that challenged the lace and frills of old stereotypes and sent women searching for more substantial, empowering images of themselves. The artist decided to use the tradition of crazy work to warn her sex against the insidious nature of the Victorian vogue, while affirming her foremothers' message that beauty could feed and comfort the spirit.

The Victorians' quilts had consisted of scraps from the opulent tables of well-to-do families: dark velvets, satins, silks, brocades, and other luxurious fabrics. They were sewn onto muslin and joined in a single kaleidoscopic design, covered with complex embroidery, ribbon, lacework, braiding, and beads. To make her own quilt an archive of old tastes and fabrics as well as new finds, Cline selected black velvet sashes, a gold satin backing, and rich modern swatches in elegant shades of teal, rose, peach, and gray. She collected such mementos as old seashells, ribbons, and pieces of antique crochet and tatting her grandmother Roberts had made. To fuse these remnants of earlier times with tangible parts of the present, she used recent newspaper articles as the interfacing for appliqués.

Cline's overall scheme for her larger-than-life composition called for a piecework of twenty fifteen-inch blocks, four in each of five variegated patterns that looked like small "crazy" collages. To "contain the madness," she worked out a grid of black velvet strips to keep the blocks separate and regimented in five horizontal rows. She also contrived a thematic device for interior order by juxtaposing symbols of women's oppression with symbols of women's power. While the individual blocks would be quilted, the full display of connected squares would be too large and heavy to stitch in this fashion, and she would devise some other way of holding the layers together. As a final touch, a single long strand of gold thread would be loosely extended across the surface to connect the blocks and reiterate their mixed messages. Crocheted to look like "a soft gold chain," it would celebrate the domestic artists' abilities and dedication while warning against excessive concern with surface appearance and showy display.

Fan block

Fan Blocks. The first four blocks run across the quilt's center and anchor the other, more complex designs. Their dominant image, a Japanese fan—created from ribbon, lamé, and brocade with touches of beadwork and lace at the edges—is Cline's cautionary reminder of the seductive decorative objects that hide women's talents as well as their anger at having to cover their strengths. At the base of the fan, a white silk butterfly formed from two female profiles or masks has been "set free" to carry our eye to a small weeping willow tree stitched in gold thread on green satin. This tree is the artist's "lamenting goddess," a figure who grieves for the lives lost behind the facades and helps younger women to escape.

Earth/Sea Blocks. The second set of five blocks, introducing the female principle of creation, embodies the tensions among competing aspects of women's identity. Using a circular form near the center to represent the female psyche, Cline added symbols of birth and new life: a starfish and seashells appear on a disk of

Earth/Sea block

green satin earth that floats on a rippling square of blue lamé water. A light chintz flower print reminiscent of nineteenth-century watercolors extends the organic dimension, while the ornamentation— the use of velvet, taffeta, moiré, and satin; the fancy beadwork, embroidery, and conspicuous over-stitching—completes the juxtaposition of natural process and artistic impulse.

Stained-Glass/Butterfly Blocks. The third set of blocks is Cline's tribute to women who heal the world's brokenness through the ministries of the arts, the church, and the medical sciences. For one of the corners, she worked out a three-layered, appliquéd stained-glass butterfly using teal satin on rose silk moiré with tight black braid for the outlines. A fusion of meanings and old and new visions, this figure serves as a metaphor for the redemptive work of putting the broken pieces back together. It acknowledges the stained glass popular in the late nineteenth century, while it invokes the emancipated butterfly images Judy Chicago set aloft in the early 1970s. Cline also enlisted a language of flowers that her Victorian counterparts used on the ornate surfaces of their crazy work. Their daisies had signified

Stained-Glass/Butterfly block

"hope," and though Cline's own hope was "somewhat wilted," she boldly embroidered a daisy on each of these blocks and had them standing tall, reaching upward and back as if braced by her foremothers' strength. Pairs of pansies, which stand for remembrance, serve to acknowledge the talents passed on by these women. Cline added, as tangible parts of this legacy, Battenburg lace and tatting from her grandmother Roberts and next to them, a small rose, the heart's timeless symbol. The ribbon attached to the rose reaches across the generations to bridge their labors—and all women's labors—of love.

Profile Blocks. While Cline's signature is on all of the squares of this crazy quilt, her face, in profile, appears on the fourth set, making it the most clearly self-referential. This cameo appearance was her way of owning the quilt, she said, of taking responsibility and credit. She also wished again to acknowledge the women of past generations who lived in her memory and in the work of her hands, so she made one of her profiles white, looking on to the light of the future, and the other black, looking back to the dusky past. Cline makes her grandmother present by using more of her elegant tatting and honors her mother by stitching a vintage Victorian flower motif. This last is embroidered in gold just above a teal square on which are sewn black and white ribbon roses and a handmade porcelain button. Pale pastels—lavender, three shades of rose, peach, mint green, and cream— and a flowered chintz print suggest distant times that are softened and sweetened by memory. Flying boldly over these quiet remnants, an appliquéd butterfly in a contemporary designer print represents the modern generation whose wings are moving us into the future.

Profile block

Web and Weaving Blocks. The fifth set of blocks displays the mixed benefits of the traditional female occupations of sewing, spinning, weaving, quilting, embroidering, and braiding. Cline's intent was to show that while these lines of work allowed women to leave their mark, they were also "stitching" them into a culture of superficial and sinister beauty. Her treatment combines polished satins with coarse, homespun cloth to remind us that many poor women have slaved in sweatshops and factories to adorn the gilded cages of rich sisters. An elegant fan embellished with braiding and beads covers part of one corner to warn yet again that a surface beauty has often concealed some ugly reality. Facing the fan from the opposite corner, a peacock feather—another ornament popular with the Victorians—reinforces the fusion of beauty and shallow vanity. Finally, as

she was reading about the Victorians' fondness for insect motifs, especially spiders, on crazy quilts, Cline discovered a bit of lore she was moved to incorporate. The Victorians like to say that a spider had saved baby Jesus from King Herod's dictum by building a web above his manger to hide him, and that a spider

Web and Weaving block

and web on a quilt would provide hope and safety for whomever the piece was made. Cline had no one person in mind to receive this quilt, but borrowed the imagery for a symbolic gift to protect and embolden all of the future's women.

Symphony in Cloth and Thread

(1992–) Series of four quilts, each approximately 56" x 56"

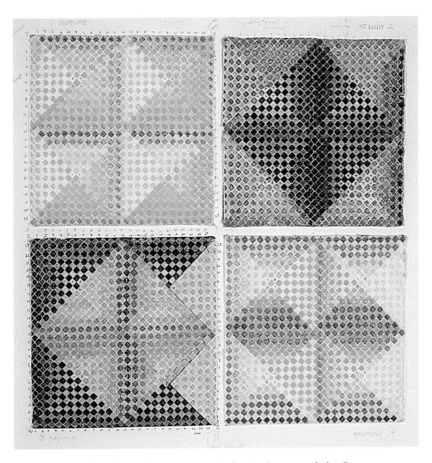

Mock-up in colored pencil on paper; clockwise from top left: Overture, Melody, Harmony, Rhythm

CLINE'S DESIRE TO FASHION a series of quilts that captured her personal struggle and the striving of all women started to germinate during the mid-1980s. The impulse appeared in embryo form in a silk-screen design called *Private Dancer* (see page 89), produced for a printmaking class in college. That project presented a set of androgynous figures in the illusion of somebody trapped behind bars reaching up and transcending them. The print pleased the artist so much that through the years she toyed with adapting it for a diptych or triptych in cloth. It was not until the autumn of 1992, however, after a year of increasing inner turmoil, that the emotional ground for this concept was ready. With her lungs failing rapidly during these months and her doctors raising the option of transplants, the artist felt trapped in a terrifying maze. To vent the intensity of what she felt and to find a way out of it, she resurrected her striving dancer as the organizing figure in an ambitious four-part *Symphony* series.

In part, this project, Cline's last, is concerned with women's inability throughout the ages to put their inner life into words because they were taught to keep their feelings in check, to hold their tongues and conform. To suggest their tightly restricted and regulated lives, she developed a set of four grids or squares pieced from one-and-one-half-inch blocks on a ninety-six-inch diagonal to form two sets of double triangles, symbols of female power and equality. With small squares arranged in subtle color progressions, each grid would draw the viewer into a pulsating optical illusion, a visual equivalent to the illusion of measured perfection that women had too often tried to achieve.

In each of the quilts, Cline phrased her visual language in musical terms showcasing vibrant scales of color, textural harmonies, and visible rhythms. Her purpose, she said, was to orchestrate a consonance of sensations that would enable "the eye to hear" her arrangement and amplify its power. She enhanced the effect with spectacular fabrics: seductive satins and taffetas of lilac and aqua; an animated, transparent moiré to catch the eye by changing from pink to gold; and a soft blend in black to lend shadow and depth.

Cline gave the four color progressions musical titles that named the stages through which her life would have to progress if it were to rise above discord and pain and emerge as a symphony. For her *Overture*, she chose a pulsating range of fiery golds and unsettling oranges, colors that capture her searing fear and disruption as well as violets that represent her feelings of vulnerability. The second quilt, *Melody*, darkens the fear by bringing in heavier blues and black, while

Harmony *(back)*, *cotton appliqués on painted silk*

Rhythm, the third piece, lightens the blues and violets to introduce hope. With *Harmony*, a study in radiant light, Cline's composition achieves the power and purity of a life redeemed.

While the artist was prepared for minor adjustments, she never expected the turn that forced a radical change. By force of long practice, Cline took it for granted that her progressions would serve as the fronts of four three-layered quilted hangings, but her soft silk backings were so seductive that they became as complex and expressive as the grids and just as demanding of our attention. This gave her the chance to try something new: a quartet of two-sided quilts with four layers, each side attached to its own thin layer of batting before being joined to its mate. On the grid side, the quilting connecting the pieced tops and batting would superimpose a large spiral so that its familiar symbolic path, which unwinds from the

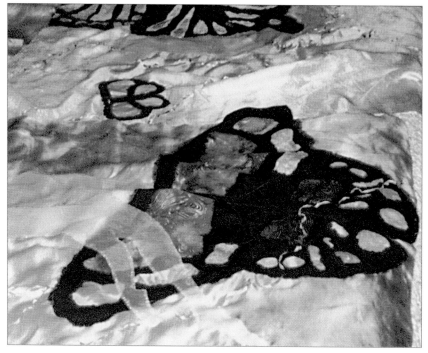

Harmony (back), *cotton appliqués on painted silk*

inside out, would etch in associations with nature's evolution and the spirit's resurrection.

Once committed to two-sided quilts, Cline began to regard the grids as the musical sheets that carried her personal song, and the panels behind them as joyful celebrations of four particular women who had achieved—as composers—significant stature in the world of music. Her research turned up very few names, however, reveal-ing instead more of women's apparent exclusion and obscurity. So her celebration became a more tempered tribute to all the world's struggling women who, like the musicians and visual artists, had been ignored or discouraged. These women were the dancing spirits who yearned to take flight when they heard songs and symphonies, but were destined to sway about "like frail whirlwinds," as Alice Walker expressed it.

In their new incarnation, Cline's old silk-screen dancers are cut out in transparent white organza and set against a gossamer of colors that she painted onto the silk. Two panels of gold and aqua and two of violet and orange repeat the tones on the opposite sides, as if they were seeping through and sustaining the dancing spirits. The spirits share their space with several large, appliquéd butterflies in the jewel-like colors of cotton batiks and couched in a softer black cotton to look like stained glass and evoke a sense of the sacred. Secured by a glowing metallic thread that lends an aura of spirituality, the striv-ing spirits mingle and seem to sway with these butterflies. Lengths of grosgrain silk ribbon, rippling from figure to figure, reinforce the connections and add an infusion of energy.

While the artist had every confidence that these *Symphony* quilts would stand on their own, she hoped that they would eventually be installed in a setting where music and lighting would let them achieve their potential for lofting a universal song.

AFTERWORD AND ACKNOWLEDGMENTS

Closure, tidy and absolute, is not the nature of books like this one. When memories carry us back to an ever receding past and words that inspire reach out to a future of readers not yet within sight, the records of human lives are put on a different footing from medical charts and the self-enclosed, linear structures of biographies. Their meanings are not beholden to narrative time and its clear-cut beginnings and endings, but rather emerge from the interplay of the fibers that bind all our human stories in one timeless volume. Defying the definitions of length and breadth, their only measure, like that of the lives they present, and like that of a masterful quilt, is their palpable integrity and the sturdiness of their seams.

Connection and not separation, recognition and not denial, are what our spirited pages have been about. The mosaic of human experience in Patricia Cline's writings and art neither glamorized nor simplified her struggle with chronic disease and despair because she refused to be hero or saint, preferring to give us her life with its natural "irregularities and imperfections." These flaws were to be expected, she said, when something is "made by hand," and they actually enhance the effect in the end.

The seams of this patchwork were reinforced by exchanges of difficult truths between friends who happily camped out in each other's lives. Sharing secrets and telling them back made us steady companions on otherwise lonely journeys. We worried about our bad habits, flaunted our eccentricities, and—despite very different religious upbringings—found we were not alone in secretly imaging God as a Spirit of Life in a female form. Our secrets now bind us together as well to a timeless community and to the ongoing story in which our readers share.

The beginnings of things have eluded us consistently. Pat's initial class journal was never recovered. Her question "Where did our friendship begin?" seemed to have no one answer and no need for any. This release from the strictures of time made it seem that her forebears had quilted forever and that her grandmothers' hands still guided her needle.

But the endings have also resisted. Though the expectation that she would soon die—at the time she asked me to speak at her funeral—was what prodded me to make this book, the idea that she would be gone and I would be saying the last words for her proved not only premature but unfounded. For despite death's proximity all through our story, not dying but living redemptively has been the operative principle. Pat will speak as long as we have eyes to read what she has to say.

Pat finally died in her sleep before dawn on November 18, 1996. It seemed fitting that there was no warning or final good-bye, for by then, those of us who were closest to her understood that her death would neither end our relationships nor close the book on her life's larger story. Like quilting, which always leaves something undone, some remnant left over, some scrap for next time, the lives that inspire and animate us never really cease, but are left here for us to continue. If we do their bidding, they live on in us. That Pat has now left us this legacy—a mandate to speak out for those who cannot, to shift our centers of gravity, to embrace the darkness as well as the light, and to put one more stitch in front of the last—is something for which we can all be grateful and celebrate.

While reading *The Color Purple* and watching Sofia and Celie make quilts on the porch, our own quilting party has grown to include many friends who helped make this book. Nancy VanCleve, a whiz of a typist as well as a faithful, discerning reader, worked miracles in turning Pat's handwritten fragments into readable pages. Carlisle

Hacker took the manuscript under her editorial wing, while photographers Katie Harper, Saj Crone, Glenn Ellis, Holly McDade, Mike Murray, and Richard Roberts provided our colorful feast of images. Grants officers Jenks McCrory of the H.W. Durham Foundation and Minna Glenn of the Memphis Arts Council not only helped us secure what money can buy but gave their priceless encouragement. Our publisher, Miriam Selby, must be thanked for the pleasure of working with her and her editor, Marge Columbus. For other support and kindnesses that made this book and its story possible, heartfelt thanks go as well to Susan Buck, Marilyn Califf, Cheryl Cornish, Evelyn Garlington, Beverly Hodorowski, Elizabeth Marshburn, Audrey May, Jean Medlick, Ann Nozawa, William Potter, John Ross, Vickie Scarborough, and all the members—past and present—of the families of Patricia Roberts Cline and Edward L. Cline, Jr.

ABOUT THE AUTHOR

Cynthia Grant Tucker was born in New York City in 1941 and attended public schools in Manhattan and Leonia, New Jersey, before moving to the Midwest for college and graduate work. She received a B.A. from Denison University (in Granville, Ohio) in 1963 and a doctorate in comparative literature from the University of Iowa in 1967. Her "real education" began, she says, when she took her first teaching job at a large, urban university in the Mid-South during an era of social upheaval. The Vietnam War and human rights movements broadened her frames of reference, shifting her academic focus to women's studies and planting a personal interest in writing biography as a way to give silenced stories a voice. Tucker's books include *Kate Freeman Clark: A Painter Rediscovered* (1981); *Healer in Harm's Way: Mary Collson, a Clergywoman in Christian Science* (1984, 1994); and *Prophetic Sisterhood: Liberal Women Ministers of the Frontier* (1990, 1994).

PHOTO CREDITS

MYTHMAKING: Heal Your Past, Claim Your Future

PATRICIA MONTGOMERY, PH.D.

Empower your future and discover the healing power of myth as you write your life story. Exercises. Thirty myths written by midlife women. "A healing, transformative tool." — **NAPRA ReVIEW** $14.95 ▪ paper ▪ 214 pp

JOURNEY IN THE MIDDLE OF THE ROAD

MURIEL MURCH

Everywoman's story of taking stock at midlife and discovering the possibilities. "A journey of discovery, of pain, and above all of love." — **The Statesman Journal** "An inspiring memoir. You won't forget this life!"— MICHAEL ONDAATJE, author, **The English Patient** $16.95 ▪ paper ▪ 196 pp

INVENTING OURSELVES AGAIN: Women Face Middle Age

JANIS FISHER CHAN

For the millions of women turning fifty this decade, a conversation among friends about their fears, feelings, discoveries about growing older. "Intimate and engaging, humorous and honest." — PATRICE WYNNE, owner, **GAIA** Bookstore $14.95 ▪ paper ▪ 202 pp

THE GODDESS SPEAKS: Myths & Meditations

DEE POTH

Capture the power of ancient goddesses by using this colorful set of meditation cards and book of stories of twenty-five goddesses. "Uncannily psychic." — **Body Mind Spirit** "Uplifting!" — MERLIN STONE $29.95 book/card set ▪ 25 cards ▪ paper ▪ 120 pp

REDEFINING SUCCESS: Women's Unique Paths

NANCY JOHNSON

Revealing stories of twenty-four remarkable women and their paths to success. Stunning photos. "The courage and generosity of these women make them modern pioneers and an inspiration." — MARGIE BOULÉ, **The Oregonian** $18.95 ▪ paper ▪ 212 pp

SACRED MYTHS: Stories of World Religions

MARILYN MCFARLANE

Benjamin Franklin Award Winner! Thirty-five best-loved stories of world religions for children 10 and up. Vivid illustrations. "Fosters tolerance and understanding." — **Publishers Weekly** "Priceless treasure, highly recommended." — **Midwest Book Review** $26.95 ▪ hardcover ▪ color ▪ 110 pp

OH BOY, OH BOY, OH BOY! Confronting Motherhood, Womanhood & Selfhood in a Household of Boys

KARIN KASDIN

Raising sons to be men who are NOT from Mars is the challenge for mothers of sons. A thoughtful, loving, and hilarious narrative of lessons learned and foibles recounted. "Kasdin tells her boys the truth about life, loves, and body noises." — LENDON H. SMITH, M.D., pediatrician, author, **How to Raise a Healthy Child** $14.95 ▪ paper ▪ 196 pp

Call Sibyl Publications 1-800-240-8566